THE ENOLA GAY

Other Aviation Titles from Potomac Books, Inc.

Aces in Command: Fighter Pilots As Combat Leaders
Walter J. Boyne

Doolittle: Aerospace Visionary
Dik Alan Daso

Flying through Time: A Journey into History in a World War II Biplane
James M. Doyle

Round-the-World Flights, Third Edition
Carroll V. Glines

Thirty Seconds over Tokyo
Ted W. Lawson

From the Flight Deck: An Anthology of the Best Writing on Carrier Warfare
Edited by Peter B. Mersky

Historic Naval Aircraft: From the Pages of Naval History Magazine
Norman Polmar

Operation Overflight: A Memoir of the V-2 Incident
Francis Gary Powers and Curt Gentry

THE ENOLA GAY

The B-29 That Dropped the Atomic Bomb on Hiroshima

NORMAN POLMAR

Potomac Books

An imprint of the University of Nebraska Press

Library of Congress Cataloging-in-Publication Data
Polmar, Norman.
    The Enola Gay : the B-29 that dropped the atomic bomb on Hiroshima / Norman Polmar.—1st ed.
        p. cm.
    Includes bibliographical references and index.
    ISBN 1-57488-859-5 (cloth : alk. paper)—ISBN 978-1-57488-836-2 (pbk. : alk. paper)
    1. Enola Gay (Bomber) 2. Hiroshima-shi (Japan)—History—Bombardment, 1945. I. Title.
    UG1249.B6P65 2004
    940.54'2521954—dc22
                        2003022646

Printed in the United States of America on acid-free paper that meets the American National Standards Institute Z39-48 Standard.

First Edition

CONTENTS

For Thomas B. Allen
who taught me so much
about writing and friendship.

DIRECTOR'S FOREWORD

On a crisp, predawn morning in March 2003, the *Enola Gay* began its final journey. The airplane's forward fuselage, still separated from its after section and wings after more than 40 years, rode a trailer out of storage in Silver Hill, Maryland, and blended in with early rush hour traffic. In the darkness, few on the bustling road to Northern Virginia could have known they were cruising alongside the past. When sunrise finally found the airplane's well-polished skin and Plexiglas windows, the nose was a few hundred feet from its new home—a unique hangar ten stories tall and the length of three football fields.

The National Air and Space Museum's new Steven F. Udvar-Hazy Center is the ultimate home for the *Enola Gay*. While the museum's flagship building in downtown Washington has been open since 1976, it can hold only about 10 percent of the national air and space collection. And a B-29 Superfortress, with a wingspan of 141 feet and a gross weight of 137,500 pounds, is too large and too heavy to be displayed intact within its galleries. The Udvar-Hazy Center allows the museum to bring the majority of its collection out of storage, with many artifacts being properly displayed for the first time. The most famous airplane from World War II deserves no less.

The *Enola Gay* was subject to the most extensive restoration effort in the museum's history. Before its disassembly in 1960, the airplane had sat outside for years at air bases—exposed in seclusion to the elements and souvenir hunters. In 1984 skilled museum technicians began the project that culminated, in 2003 on the floor of the new center's aviation hangar, in the arduous reunion of fuselage sections, wings, landing gear, engines, propellers, and vertical stabilizer.

In total, hundreds of thousands of museum staff hours were spent bringing the airplane back as closely as possible to its 1945 condition. All metal surfaces were cleaned and coated with preservative. Missing equipment was replaced. Even Boeing logo caps from the period were tracked down for the center of the cockpit control wheels. In short, the *Enola Gay* was made ready for its final role: bearing witness to the turning point of the 20th Century.

Because of the work of some very talented men and women, future generations will sense first-hand the unalterable significance of the B-29 used to drop the first atomic bomb in war. As the museum's deputy director and World War II fighter ace Donald Lopez once summed up the aircraft and its times, "It is a major artifact. It's history. It happened."

The public is finally seeing the *Enola Gay* as it was in those final days of the world's worst conflict. Let's learn from it.

General John R. Dailey, U.S. Marine Corps (Ret.)
Director
National Air and Space Museum

CURATOR'S VIEWPOINT

The union of the Boeing B-29 Superfortress with the atomic bomb not only contributed to the defeat of Japan, but also established the foundation of strategic aviation in American Cold War policy for the following four and a half decades. Moreover, President Harry S. Truman's order to drop the atomic bombs on Japan reinforced the most fundamental of American military traditions: civil control over the armed forces.

The B-29 was a technological marvel for its time, although it was initially plagued by severe engine problems. It was a monster of an aircraft with respect to size, heavily armed with defensive guns, comfortable by World War II aircraft standards, and capable of carrying large bomb loads to distant targets. The aircraft proved effective in attacking Japan with conventional and incendiary bombs, in daylight and at night, as well as in sowing naval mines in coastal waters. Although the development of jet-propelled aircraft—including bombers—was well underway by the time that the B-29 *Enola Gay* dropped the atomic bomb on Hiroshima in August 1945, the B-29 would remain in first-line service as a bomber for another decade.

Stories of the *Enola Gay* and the overall development and operations of the B-29 are well worth revisiting because of the military and technological, as well as the political, implications of those efforts. This book effort effectively links those stories. While some aspects of the stories remain controversial even today, there can be no question that the *Enola Gay*, the men who maintained and flew her, the men and women who built her, and the bomb that she released over Hiroshima on August 6, 1945, changed the nature of warfare for all time.

Dik Daso
Curator of Modern Military Aircraft
National Air and Space Museum

AUTHOR'S PERSPECTIVE

The *Enola Gay* is a historic aircraft, representing both the world's entry into the atomic age and an important step in the development of U.S. military aviation. It is also the largest combat aircraft in the collection of the National Air and Space Museum.

The world entered the atomic age in 1945, when the United States and its allies were locked in a desperate war against Japan. The first atomic bomb was detonated on July 16, 1945, in the New Mexico wilderness atop a 103-foot steel tower. Shortly before dawn a so-called Fat Man bomb was exploded, producing a blinding explosion equivalent to the force of 18.6 kilotons (i.e., 18,600 tons) of TNT.

Three weeks later, in the predawn darkness of August 6, the B-29 *Enola Gay* of the 509th Composite Group took off from the island of Tinian in the Mariana Islands carrying a Little Boy atomic bomb. The aircraft flew 1,500 miles to the Japanese city of Hiroshima and released the bomb. The Little Boy exploded with the force of 12.5 kilotons of TNT, destroying the city. That was the first time an atomic bomb was used in combat. Thus, the *Enola Gay* and her crew of 12 officers and enlisted men earned their place in aviation history. But so did the B-29. It was the most effective bomber aircraft flown in World War II in terms of performance and defensive capability.

Three days later another B-29—named *Bockscar*—dropped a Fat Man atomic bomb on the Japanese city of Nagasaki. The Japanese government surrendered on August 15, Tokyo time.

Almost 4,000 B-29s were produced, and they saw extensive combat in the Far East and Pacific during World War II and, subsequently, in the Korean War. They also flew in photo- and weather-reconnaissance roles, performed various research activities, and served as aerial tankers, search-and-rescue aircraft, and airborne monitoring platforms to detect nuclear detonations by the Soviet Union. Britain's Royal Air Force flew the B-29, and the Soviet and Chinese air forces flew a carbon copy of the aircraft developed by Andrei Tupolev.

Aviation historian Peter M. Bowers wrote in *Boeing Aircraft Since 1916*:

> If for no other reason than the part it played in bringing an early end to the Pacific phase of [World War] II, the B-29 Superfortress must be recognized as one of the outstanding

aeroplanes in the history of military aviation. Aside from its tactical performance, the B-29 deserves recognition for the contribution that it made toward subsequent design and for the truly heroic development programme that in four years designed, built, tested, and perfected one of the most complex pieces of movable machinery ever made up to the time and trained the crews that put it in action over ranges never before attained in combat operations.[1]

Norman Polmar

AUTHOR'S PERSPECTIVE

ACKNOWLEDGMENTS

This book was produced under the direction of Ted A. Maxwell, associate director of the National Air and Space Museum. Several members of the museum staff provided invaluable assistance in the research, writing, and editing of this manuscript and in photograph selection, especially Dominick A. Pisano, then chairman of the Aeronautics Division, and several of his curators, especially Robert van der Linden and Dik Daso. Dana Bell, Phil Edwards, Dan Hagedorn, Kristine Kaske, Brian Nicklas, and Mark Taylor of the Archives Division provided considerable help and support. Eric Long furnished the color photography of the *Enola Gay*. Also helpful were Al Christman, the biographer of Admiral William S. Parsons, and Robert Standish Norris, biographer of General Leslie R. Groves.

Patricia Graboske of the National Air and Space Museum and Richard (Rick) Russell of Brassey's, Inc., made this book a reality. Dorothy Altmiller, managing editor at Brassey's, saw to it that the book was worthy of its subject.

GLOSSARY

AAF	Army Air Forces
AEW	Airborne Early Warning
AFB	Air Force Base
FEAF	Far East Air Force (U.S.)
FICON	Fighter Conveyor
KT	Kiloton (equivalent of 1,000 tons of TNT)
LRA	Long-Range Aviation (Soviet)
RAF	Royal Air Force (U.K.)
RCM	Radar Countermeasures
USA	U.S. Army
USAF	U.S. Air Force
VHB	Very-Heavy Bomber
VLR	Very-Long Range

THE ENOLA GAY

THE B-29 SUPERFORTRESS

1

The B-29 Superfortress was the most effective bomber of any nation to see combat in World War II. The aircraft was developed as a strategic bomber to carry out long-range, high-altitude, daylight bombing attacks.

The origins of the B-29 can be traced to a series of bomber aircraft produced by the Boeing Airplane Company in the 1920s and 1930s. In the aftermath of World War I, several aviation zealots proclaimed the decisive role of aircraft in winning future wars through the bombardment of an enemy's homeland. The best known of these men were Italian theorist Guilio Douhet, Britain's Hugh Trenchard, and William (Billy) Mitchell, the U.S. Army aviation commander in Europe at the end of World War I. These men believed that strategic bombing could force an enemy to surrender without the costly ground and naval campaigns that had been fought in World War I.

Following their precepts, the air services of several countries began the development of long-range bombers. In the United States several aircraft manufacturers initiated bomber development in this period, among them the Boeing firm, which had built its first aircraft in 1916.[1] In the late 1920s Boeing designed one of the early

modern bomber aircraft, the firm's Model 214/215, a twin-engine, low-wing monoplane with an internal bomb bay. The U.S. Army purchased two bomber prototypes, with the aircraft Model 215, designated Y1B-9, being the first to fly, in 1931. Although those planes were preceded by the Douglas B-7 series as the Army's first twin-engine monoplane bomber, the Boeing Y1B-9 was generally recognized as a revolutionary bomber design because of its aerodynamic and structural features.

Only a few production B-9 bombers were built, but they were the basis for the subsequent streamlined bombers produced by Boeing. In response to the Army's next large-bomber competition, Boeing produced the XB-15, the first U.S. four-engine monoplane bomber, which flew in 1937. It was the largest and heaviest airplane built in the United States at that time. (The Russian designer Igor Sikorsky had designed and flown the world's first four-engine aircraft, the *Grand*, in 1913. His first four-engine bomber, the *Il'ya Muromets*, flew the following year, and 79 were produced; they saw extensive combat in World War I and the Russian Civil War.[2]

But even before the XB-15 flew, Boeing initiated a smaller and more advanced design, the four-engine Model 299. The prototype

A Boeing B-17G Flying Fortress over the United States in 1944. The B-17 was the immediate predecessor of the B-29 and, although a rugged and relatively long-range bomber, its performance and survivability were far surpassed by the B-29. (U.S. Navy)

came the most famous Allied bomber of World War II. The B-17 flew in all theaters of the war and was in combat from the time of the Japanese attacks on Pearl Harbor and the Philippines on December 7–8, 1941, through the end of the war in Europe in May 1945.

The B-17 was not the fastest U.S. bomber; nor did it have the largest bomb capacity or the longest range; nor was it produced in the greatest numbers. Rather, its great fame came from an effective Army Air Forces (AAF) public relations program and from its wide use. From the combat perspective, the B-17 was able to sustain considerable damage and still fly and had a heavier defensive gun armament than any bomber aircraft built up to that time.

A total of 12,726 B-17s were built by three firms by the end of the war: Boeing (6,981), Douglas (2,995), and Lockheed-Vega (2,750). The peak AAF inventory for B-17s was 6,043 aircraft in September 1943. At that time there were 33 B-17 groups overseas, as compared with 45½ groups of B-24 Libera-

flew (unarmed) for 2,000 miles nonstop at an average speed of 252 mph—an impressive performance. The Army ordered 13 service test aircraft, designated Y1B-17. Large-scale production got underway just before the United States entered World War II in December 1941.

As the B-17, the aircraft was named the Flying Fortress and be-

tor bombers. Yet, U.S. B-17 Flying Fortresses dropped 640,036 tons of bombs on European targets from 1942 to 1945; B-24s dropped 452,508 tons. Further, B-24s continued in service in the Pacific after the end of the war in Europe, while the B-17s were retired from front-line service immediately after the European war. (Between 1940 and the end of the war, 18,190 Consolidated B-24s were built—more than any other U.S. military aircraft in history; another 740 PB4Y-2 Privateers—low-level, maritime patrol aircraft based on the B-24—were built for the Navy.)

In 1938 the Army Air Corps asked Boeing to undertake a design study of an improved B-17 with pressurized crew compartments (for high-altitude flight) and a tricycle landing gear. A pressurized aircraft would provide a more comfortable environment for the crew on long missions and would enable the plane to operate at higher altitudes, where it would be less vulnerable to enemy fighters and anti-aircraft fire. This design was designated Boeing Model 334 and was developed with company funds.

In the meantime, Lieutenant General Henry H. (Hap) Arnold, the head of the Army Air Corps, had become alarmed by the growing war clouds in Europe and by the Japanese military campaign in China.[3] In May 1939 he established a special board, chaired by Brigadier General Walter G. Kilner, to make recommendations for the long-term needs of the Army Air Corps. The famed aviator Charles Lindbergh was a member of the committee.[4] Lindbergh had recently toured German aircraft factories and Luftwaffe bases, where he had been convinced that Germany was well ahead of its potential European adversaries in aviation developments.

In its June 1939 report, the Kilner board recommended that several new, long-range, medium and heavy bombers be developed. Hastened by a new urgency caused by the recent outbreak of war in Europe, General Arnold on November 10, 1939, requested War Department and congressional permission to contract with major aircraft companies for studies of a Very-Long Range (VLR) bomber. Congressional authorization was forthcoming, and in January of 1940 the Army issued the formal requirements for the VLR "super bomber."

B-17E Flying Fortresses over Europe. Contrails from other B-17s and escorting fighters fill the sky above these bombers. Although their effectiveness was limited, the U.S. daylight bombing effort tied up massive amounts of German defensive guns, fighters, and troops. (AAF)

The Army's 1940 super bomber was to have a maximum speed of at least 400 mph and a range of 5,333 miles while carrying a 2,000-pound bomb load to one-half that distance. By comparison, the B-17B, the first production model of the Flying Fortress, could fly at 292 mph and travel about 700 miles to reach a target, drop 2,000 pounds of bombs, and return to base. As lessons from the European war were analyzed, requirements were added to the B-29 for heavier defensive armament, additional armor, and self-sealing fuel tanks.

The super bomber specifications were embodied in Request for Data R-40B and Specification XC-218. On January 29, 1940, the War Department formally issued Data R-40B—the requirement for the super bomber—and circulated it to the Boeing, Consolidated, Douglas, and Lockheed firms. The specification was revised in April to incorporate the lessons learned in early European combat and now included more defensive armament, armor, and fuel tanks that were self-sealing against battle damage.

All four aircraft firms responded to the Army's requirement: Boeing with the B-29, Lockheed with the XB-30 bomber variant of its futuristic Constellation transport aircraft, Douglas with a series of designs carrying the designation XB-31, and Convair with the XB-32, an enlarged and improved version of the firm's highly successful B-24 Liberator.

The Boeing Company had a leg up on its competition, since it had already been thinking along the very same lines as the super bomber specification. On September 6, 1940, a contract was awarded to Boeing for $3,615,095 to construct two prototype B-29 aircraft, plus a static test model. A third flying model was soon added. Thus began the B-29 program.

Even before the first XB-29 took to the air, the Army was sufficiently impressed by the Boeing design to place orders for 250 production aircraft. In January 1942, a month after the United States entered World War II, the number was increased to 500 aircraft. In addition to the new government-owned Boeing plant in Wichita, Kansas, new aircraft factories operated by Bell at Marietta, Georgia, and by Martin at Omaha, Nebraska, would produce the B-29. This was a remarkable production effort for an aircraft that had not yet flown!

WHAT'S IN A NAME?

Initially, the B-29 Superfortress was referred to as a "heavy bomber." Subsequently, the AAF indiscriminately used the terms Very-Long Range (VLR) bomber and Very-Heavy Bomber (VHB) to describe both the B-29 and the B-32 Dominator. The latter term was the official designation of bomber units like the 313rd Bombardment Wing.

The term VLR was favored in most early AAF planning papers and was in fact more appropriate as the B-29's range, rather than its bomb load, was more significant.

The surviving B-29s and derivative B-50s were reclassified as medium bombers in 1948 (at which time only the new B-36 Peacemaker was classified as VHB).

B-17 AND B-29 CHARACTERISTICS

	B-17B	B-17E	B-17G	B-29
First flight	1939	1941	1943	1942
Crew	9	10	10	11
Empty weight (lbs)	27,652	33,279	36,135	69,610
Gross weight (lbs)	37,997	53,000	65,500	105,000‡
Maximum speed (mph)	292	317	287	365
Service ceiling (ft)	30,600	36,600	35,600	31,850
Maximum range (mi)	1,400	2,000*	2,000*	3,900
Bomb load (lbs)	2,000	4,000	6,000†	10,000#

Notes: *Range with bomb load shown carried to one-half the distance.
†Maximum bomb load was 9,600 pounds.
‡Gross weight was increased to 140,000 pounds in post–World War II modifications.
#Maximum bomb load was 20,000 pounds.

The XB-29 first flew on September 21, 1942, with Boeing's chief test pilot, Edmund T. Allen, at the controls.[5] It was a remarkable aircraft in terms of its design, size, and potential combat capabilities. It was the largest combat aircraft to fly in World War II, with a greater range and payload than any other bomber, with the exception that the British Lancaster could carry a heavier bomb load for shorter distances.

The four-engine B-29 was a streamlined bomber; its maximum takeoff weight was 135,000 pounds, including up to ten tons of bombs; the B-17G carried a maximum of three tons. With a several-ton bomb load, the new bomber could fly to targets 1,500 miles away, more than twice the combat radius of the B-17. And the B-29 had a defensive armament of eight or ten .50-caliber machine guns in four remote-control turrets, plus a tail turret mounting two additional machine guns and, in some aircraft, one 20-millimeter cannon. The remote control meant that gunners in optimum positions to observe enemy aircraft could control various combinations of guns to defend the aircraft.

MASS PRODUCTION

Production of the B-29 was accelerated. At the time of the first XB-29 flight there were 1,664 aircraft on order. Placing an aircraft in quantity production before even the prototype had flown was "a radical departure from long established custom—called familiarly 'the three-billion-dollar gamble'—[that] not only involved a huge financial risk, [but] threatened also to disrupt schedules of desperately needed aircraft models already in production," according to the official U.S. AAF history.[6] The extent of the risk was evidenced by the fact that the materials required for one B-29 airframe, measured by weight, equaled the amount needed for 11 P-51 Mustang fighters.

The first production B-29 rolled off the assembly line in July 1943. Following test flights, several technical bugs had to be worked out

A Boeing B-29 Superfortress in flight, showing the impressive size and streamlined lines of the ultimate piston-engine bomber of the war. The planes were plagued with mechanical problems, but massive stocks of parts (especially engines) and maintenance personnel kept them flying. (Boeing/NASM)

of the B-29, and the crash of the second prototype because of an engine fire further delayed the program. Even after the plane entered production, flight and maintenance crews had to be trained, the B-29 units established, spare parts stockpiled, and a myriad of other actions undertaken before the aircraft could be ready for combat. At that time B-17 Flying Fortress and B-24 Liberator bombers were being used in the Pacific, Mediterranean, and European theaters. The AAF staff felt that it would be difficult to introduce another heavy bomber into the Mediterranean and European areas because of the massive base and logistics requirements to support each bomber type. And, more importantly, the great range of the B-29 would be more valuable across the broad reaches of the China-Burma-India and Pacific Ocean theaters.

By 1943 U.S. military planners were considering a number of potential bases for the strategic bombing of Japan. The bases considered by American planners for the B-29, which could become available for use in 1944, included the Mariana Islands, Soviet Siberia, Manchuria, Korea, Formosa, and the Philippines. The plan adopted in mid-1943 for attacks on Japan called for basing the B-29s in China and, after its capture, on the island of Formosa (now Taiwan).

In November 1943 the U.S. Joint Planning Staff completed a plan known as the "Early Sustained Bombing of Japan." The plan—given the code name Matterhorn—advocated bringing the four-engine "Superforts" into the war against Japan as soon as possible.[7] On November 11, President Franklin D. Roosevelt formally approved the plan.

The first B-29s to go overseas were secretly flown over the Atlantic Ocean, across North Africa, and then to India. At the same time, one B-29 was sent openly to England as a feint to mislead enemy spies. Matterhorn would be carried out from forward bases in those portions of China held by the nationalist armies of Chiang Kai-shek. The main B-29 bases and their massive logistic support structure were established in India. By May 1944, after vast expenditures of U.S. funds and the labor of some 400,000 Chinese, four bases for B-29s had been built in the Chengtu area of China, as were several bases for fighter aircraft to protect the bomber fields. Thousands of support personnel—mechanics, armorers, cooks, bakers, and warehousemen—had to be brought to the bases in China, along with spare parts (including replacement engines), bombs, provisions, and even fuel. For example, to launch an attack with 100 B-29s from the Chinese bases required some 2,300 tons of flown-in supplies, besides what the bombers themselves had to carry when they flew into China from the rear bases in India.

The first combat mission of the war for B-29s of the XX Bomber Command was against Japanese installations in Bangkok, Thailand, on June 5, 1944. The planes took off from airfields in India and used landing fields in China as staging bases. Those B-29s flew additional raids against Japanese targets in Southeast Asia and on the night of June 15–16, 1944, made their first strike against the Japanese home islands. The target was the Yawata steel works on Kyushu, the southernmost island. The plant produced an estimated 24 percent of Japan's rolled steel.

Seventy-five B-29s were dispatched on the Yawata raid. One crashed on takeoff, and ten more were forced to abort their missions shortly after taking off and returned to their bases. The round-trip flight of 3,200 miles restricted the planes to only two tons of bombs each, and the long distance required the planes to fly individually in a stream, rather than in formation, to avoid using up fuel to form up into large plane formations. Also, the strike was flown at night to reduce vulnerability to Japanese fighters and anti-aircraft guns. Forty-seven B-29s reached the target. There was some fighter opposition and anti-aircraft fire. Despite some damage, none of the planes was downed by enemy fire, although three more were lost on the return flight.

A photo-reconnaissance B-29 sent over Yawata a few days later found the damage was "unimportant," according to the official AAF

A formation of B-29s approaching their base in India. From the outset the B-29 force was assigned to the China-Burma-India theater because of the perceived difficulties in introducing the bomber into the European-Mediterranean areas and the need for the plane's long range in Asia and the Pacific. (AAF)

A B-29 of the 444th Bomb Group at a base in China. Missions flown from China were difficult to support because of logistics, the lack of base facilities, and other factors. Only after the capture of the Marianas in the summer of 1944 could effective B-29 bases be established for the aerial bombardment of Japan. (AAF)

B-29s of the 29th Bomb Group are massed on Guam's North Field. When the war ended, the Army Air Forces had 40 groups of B-29s, of which 21 groups with almost 1,500 aircraft were based in the Marianas and on Okinawa. The Okinawa-based B-29s were a component of the Eighth Air Force under Lieutenant General James (Jimmy) Doolittle. (AAF)

bomb targets in Japan. But, given the logistics required to support the B-29s and their ineffective high-altitude daylight bombing tactics, raids from Chinese bases were hardly worth the effort, and air strategists finally realized that only the Mariana Islands in the western Pacific could provide effective bases for B-29s.

U.S. Marines and soldiers made amphibious assaults against Guam, Tinian, and Saipan in mid-1944.[9] With their capture the B-29s would have airfields only some 1,500 miles from Tokyo. There was little threat of Japanese air or ground attack in the Marianas, and cargo ships and tankers could bring in the bombs, supplies, parts, and fuel without the cost of and time needed for air transport to the B-29 bases in China. (The small Marianas island of Rota remained in Japanese hands until the end of the war, and there were a few Japanese holdouts on the islands that had been captured by U.S. troops.)

The first B-29 bomber strike from the Marianas was flown on October 28, 1944, against the Japanese submarine base on the island of Truk. Subsequently, large B-29 raids began against Japan from the Marianas, a 13-hour round-trip flight. These were initially high-altitude, daylight strikes that had limited success. Although the B-29 was designed for daylight precision bombing from 30,000 feet or above, those early raids against Japan accomplished little, despite the tremendous B-29 effort. The B-29s were hampered by difficulties with their radar, inadequate weather reports, and the unexpected high

history. Only one hit in the main plant area was scored—of the 376 500-pound bombs dropped on the target that night.[8]

Planes from the XX Bomber Command continued to strike Japanese targets in the Southeast Asia area and periodically returned to winds (up to 230 mph) encountered over Japan. The last meant that a B-29 bombing downwind could have a relative ground speed of 550 mph, which was beyond the computing capability of the Norden bombsight.

Early in 1945, Major General Curtis LeMay, commander of the XXI Bomber Command in the Marianas, initiated low-level, night incendiary raids against Japanese cities from an altitude of 5,000 feet. This was a complete reversal of the AAF doctrine of high-altitude, daylight precision bombing. LeMay wrote that because of the bad weather over Japanese targets, "During my first six weeks here we had one visual shot at the target. This was primarily the reason I lowered the altitude for our incendiary attacks."[10]

The first firebomb raid was made by 279 B-29s against Tokyo on the night of March 9–10, 1945. Fierce fires took hold and, fanned by 20 mph winds, precipitated a firestorm. About 16 square miles of the city were almost completely destroyed, and over one million people—one-seventh of the capital's population—lost their homes. A reported 83,783 people were killed, and many thousands more were injured.[11]

Low-level incendiary and medium-altitude precision bombing raids continued with increasing numbers of B-29s flying from airfields on Guam, Saipan, and Tinian. The largest B-29 raid of the war came on August 1, 1945, when 836 aircraft were launched from the Marianas with 784 reaching their targets in Japan. In addition

Replacement engines are stacked at North Field on Guam in the Marianas, awaiting installation in B-29s of the 19th Bomb Group. Engines burned out on a regular basis during the approximately 13-hour flights from the Marianas to the Tokyo area, causing the loss of several B-29s and requiring engine replacements. (AAF)

to dropping almost 170,000 tons of conventional bombs during 14 months of war, B-29s dropped over 12,000 aerial mines in Japanese and Korean waters to stop coastal shipping.

Combat losses of B-29s during those raids were relatively few: 147 aircraft lost to Japanese fighters or anti-aircraft fire. Another 267 B-29s were classified as operational losses, brought down by mechanical problems, crashing on taking off or landing, or running out of fuel during the long, over-water flights. By the end of the war, 3,015 B-29 crewmen were casualties—killed, missing, and

A ground crewman repaints markings on the tail fin of a B-29 from the 314th Bomb Wing on Guam. The tail gun position and its twin .50-caliber machine guns are visible as is the after ventral turret. The centralized, remote fire-control system made the B-29 the best-defended bomber of the war. (AAF)

injured. In return, several hundred Japanese fighters were shot down. (B-29 gunners claimed more than 2,000 aerial kills during the war.)

In mid-1945 the AAF had 40 groups of B-29s; 21 with almost 1,500 aircraft were at bases in the western Pacific. Not only was the Twentieth Air Force flying B-29s from the Mariana Islands, but in July 1945, Lieutenant General James (Jimmy) Doolittle, leader of the historic carrier raid on Japan in April 1942 and commander of the Eighth Air Force in Europe since January 1945, arrived on Okinawa.[12] His Eighth Air Force—which had become synonymous with the B-17 bombing campaign against German-held Europe—was being returned to the United States and retrained in B-29s. With these two U.S. air forces, the strategic bombers attacking Japan in late 1945 and into 1946 would number some 2,000 B-29s.

(In addition, Britain's Royal Air Force was deploying the so-called Tiger Force to Okinawa to participate in the air war against Japan. Their Lancaster Mark VII bombers were to begin arriving on Okinawa's crowded airfields about September 1945. Between 30 and 36 squadrons, each with 16 aircraft, were to comprise the Tiger Force, adding a few hundred more bombers to the air assault on Japan.)

And, at the Allied planning conference at Yalta on the Black Sea in February 1945, Soviet premier Josef Stalin had acceded to President Roosevelt's request for two bases in the Soviet Far East for B-29 operations. Although logistic support of B-29s in eastern Siberia would have been very difficult, if

B-29s from the 497th Bomb Group lined up at Isley Field on Saipan, awaiting their turn at taking off for a strike on the Japanese home islands. In the largest bomber strike of the Pacific war, on August 1, 1945, 836 B-29s took off from the Marianas with 784 reaching their targets in Japan. (AAF)

not impossible, those airfields could have served as emergency, or shuttle-bombing, bases for the U.S. planes.

These B-29 and Lancaster operations were in addition to the Far East Air Forces (FEAF) under Lieutenant General George C. Kenney. With the Fifth and Thirteenth Air Forces, the FEAF, flying from the Philippines, Okinawa, and Guam, had medium bombers and light bombers, as well as four-engine B-24 Liberators and B-32 Dominators. Finally, the U.S. and British carrier forces in the western Pacific could put more than 1,000 planes over the Japanese home islands.

Thus, by September 1945 the aggregate of Allied bombs

dropped on Japan per month was expected to reach 100,000 tons. In January 1946 it was to reach 170,000 tons, and by March 1946, 220,000 tons of bombs per month were to fall on Japanese targets. However, this massive, conventional bombing—conducted mostly by B-29 Superfortress bombers—was not to be. In August 1945, two specially modified B-29s each dropped a single atomic bomb on a Japanese city. The devastation wrought by those planes led to a rapid end to the war. The plane that dropped the first atomic bomb was named *Enola Gay*.

Incendiary bombs rain down on a Japanese city from B-29s of the 500th Bomb Group based on Saipan. High visibility made it easier for the aircraft to form up after takeoff from the several B-29 bases in the Marianas. (AAF)

THE *ENOLA GAY*

Aircraft serial number 44–86292—later named *Enola Gay*—was delivered to the U.S. Army Air Forces (AAF) by the Martin aircraft factory in Omaha, Nebraska, on May 18, 1945.[1] By that time B-29 production lines were working around the clock at the Boeing-operated plants in Wichita, Kansas, and Renton (Seattle), Washington, and at the Bell plant in Marietta, Georgia, as well as at the Martin factory.

Aircraft No. 44–86292 was built as a standard B-29 Superfortress. The B-29 featured a long, circular fuselage, with an all-Plexiglas nose (in place of the stepped cockpit of earlier Boeing bombers). The large, vertical tail assembly was smoothly faired into the fuselage. The B-29 wings measured just over 141 feet from tip to tip, with the leading edge swept back seven degrees. Fuel tanks were fitted in the inner portions of the wing to increase range—the wing tanks carried 6,800 gallons of fuel, and two fuselage tanks carried another 2,560 gallons.

The wing was one of the most difficult aspects of the B-29 design. It had to have low drag at cruising speeds (to increase range) with good high-speed and stall characteristics. But the wing loading

The name *Enola Gay* was given to B-29 No. 44–86292 on the eve of the atomic bombing of Hiroshima. That aircraft, shown here on display at the Steven F. Udvar-Hazy Center at Dulles International Airport, is the most famous of the almost 4,000 B-29s produced during World War II. (Eric Long/NASM)

was projected to be so high that special features were needed to prevent the aircraft's having a prohibitively high landing speed.[2] This was accomplished by using the largest wing flaps ever developed to increase the lift coefficient of the wing during landing and takeoff. These flaps added 20 percent to the overall wing area when fully extended. The B-29 wing design was tested in flight by substituting quarter-size wing mockups for the regular wings of a Fairchild PT-19A trainer.

The construction of the B-29 was fairly conventional, being all metal throughout, but with fabric-covered control surfaces. Each undercarriage unit had dual, instead of single, wheels. A retractable tail skid was provided for tail protection during nose-high takeoffs and landings.

From the outset it was recognized that the B-29 would require four powerful engines. Boeing's first four-engine modern bomber, the XB-15, had been seriously underpowered, and it was decided to ensure that the B-29 had engines that could provide the required performance. After several false starts, the decision was made to power the B-29 with the Wright R-3350, the most powerful—and most complicated—piston engine yet built. This was an 18-cylinder radial engine that produced 2,200 horsepower.[3]

Unfortunately, the early R-3350 engines were subject to chronic overheating and were especially prone to catching fire upon the slightest provocation. During the first 23 test flights of the XB-29, chief test pilot Ed Allen was able to log only 27 hours in the air. Sixteen engines had to be changed, 19 exhaust systems had to be revised, and 22 carburetors had to be replaced. There were also problems with the fuel mixture. Even after the engine problems had been solved, the engines required extensive maintenance and frequent replacement.

Each R-3350 engine turned a four-blade propeller in the production aircraft, after experiments with three-blade propellers in the XB-29 and some YB-29s. The 16-foot, 7-inch diameter of the four-blade propellers required a new propeller gear ratio for optimum per-

formance, with the propeller having 35 revolutions for every 100 revolutions of the engine crankshaft. As a result, the B-29 had the slowest-turning propellers of any major military aircraft. The power plants could move the B-29 at combat weight—just over 101,000 pounds—at 399 mph at 30,000 feet. The plane's combat radius was listed as 1,955 miles at 253 mph with 10,000 pounds of bombs.

The B-29 was the world's first production bomber with fully pressurized crew compartments. This permitted the crew to fly and work at much higher altitudes and, when not in combat, to fly without oxygen masks. In combat masks would be worn, however, because of the danger that battle damage could destroy the aircraft's pressurization. Full pressurization of the fuselage was considered impractical because of the need to open the bomb bays during high-altitude flight to release bombs. Accordingly, there were three pressurized crew compartments within the fuselage:

1. *Nose compartment:* The bombardier sat in the nose with his bombsight and a remote-control gun sight. The pilot and copilot sat side by side above and behind the bombardier. The flight engineer, radio operator, and navigator sat immediately behind the pilots' positions.
2. *Mid-fuselage compartment:* The second pressurized compartment housed three gunners and the radar operator.
3. *Tail turret:* The tail gunner sat in a separate pressurized compartment in the extreme rear of the aircraft. He could enter or leave the compartment only during unpressurized flight.

Later, some aircraft would additionally be fitted with Radar Countermeasures (RCM) equipment to detect Japanese radar emissions; the RCM equipment and operator were located in the mid-fuselage section. (The RCM operator brought the B-29's crew up to 12 men.)

The nose and mid-fuselage compartments were connected by a narrow, fully pressurized tunnel passing over the bomb bays to enable crew members to change positions during pressurized flight.

The cockpit of the *Enola Gay* showing the pilot (left) and copilot positions, and beyond them, in the nose, the bombardier's position. In addition to the pilot and copilot, the flight engineer was vital to flying the aircraft; seated behind the pilot, he had the majority of the engine controls and most of the electrical and mechanical system controls. (Eric Long/NASM)

The tail gunner's pressurized position was isolated from the rest of the aircraft.

The twin bomb bays—forward and aft of the wing spar—together could accommodate a maximum of 20,000 pounds of general-purpose bombs in several combinations:

4	4,000 pounders
8	2,000 pounders
12	1,000 pounders
40	500 pounders

Incendiaries could be substituted for general-purpose bombs. For example, for the incendiary raids against Japan that began in

The Norden bombsight now in the *Enola Gay* is the actual device used by the bombardier, Major Thomas W. (Tom) Ferebee, to release the Little Boy atomic bomb over Hiroshima. Major General Leslie Groves, head of the atomic bomb program, wanted the B-29s to release their bombs visually with the Norden bombsight, rather than by radar. (Eric Long/NASM)

March 1945, each B-29 could carry 180 70-pound M47 napalm-filled bombs or 24 500-pound clusters of M69 magnesium bombs.[4] The release of bombs was controlled through an intervalometer to preserve aircraft balance as the bombs fell away by alternating release between the forward and after bays.

The B-29s modified to the Silverplate configuration for the atomic bomb program retained only their twin .50-caliber tail guns. The circle-R insignia of the 6th Bomb Group was used on the atomic missions, not the arrowhead within a circle of the 509th Composite Group. (Eric Long/NASM)

Each B-29 was fitted with the Norden bombsight and either the AN/APQ-7 Eagle or AN/APQ-13 radar to assist in navigation over ground and target recognition.[5] (A few aircraft also were fitted with the AN/APQ-15 tail gun aiming radar, but that short-range device was difficult to operate and maintain.)

The aircraft's defensive armament was the heaviest of any bomber yet built. The B-29 was the world's first production aircraft to make extensive use of remotely controlled defensive guns and a central fire-control system. A remotely controlled armament system was adopted in place of manned turrets (as in the B-17 and B-24), which were not practical for the altitudes at which the B-29 was to operate.[6]

Four gun turrets were provided, two on top of the fuselage (dorsal) and two beneath the fuselage (ventral), in addition to the tail turret. The bombardier and three gunners could control the four dorsal and ventral turrets, each of which contained two .50-caliber machine guns with 500 rounds of ammunition per barrel. The tail turret initially had two .50-caliber guns with 500 rounds per barrel. Subsequently, some production aircraft were additionally fitted with a 20-millimeter tail cannon, while the forward dorsal turret was modified to house four .50-caliber guns. Those brought the B-29's firepower up to 13 guns.

When the AAF accepted Martin-built B-29 No. 44–86292 in May 1945, most of those who observed the brief ceremony assumed that the aircraft would quickly be sent to the Mariana Islands or Okinawa to take part in the conventional bombing of the Japanese home islands. Instead, the aircraft would become part of the Silverplate program.

The U.S. atomic bomb effort had formally begun in

June 1942. Given high priority and massive resources, the project had progressed to the point in August 1944 that the head of the Manhattan Project, Major General Leslie R. Groves, advised the AAF that he expected the first atomic bomb of the uranium type (Little Boy) to be ready in June 1945 and thought the first plutonium bomb (Fat Man) might be available as early as January 1945. Groves would later write, "In order to avoid any possible unnecessary delay in the use of the bomb, the dates that I gave [the AAF] were in advance of my actual expectations."[7]

In response to urging from Groves, the AAF began planning for the delivery of the atomic bomb against targets in Germany or Japan using the B-29 Superfortress. Earlier, there had been some doubt that even the B-29 was large enough to carry an atomic bomb. Some consideration was given to obtaining British Lancaster bombers, the only aircraft capable of carrying the 12,000-pound Tallboy and the gigantic 22,000-pound Grand Slam, the world's largest bombs.[8]

THE SILVERPLATE PROGRAM

In response, the AAF initiated the Silverplate program to ensure that U.S. bombers would carry the atomic bombs. General Groves had originally asked that three bombers be modified to carry the bombs. In the late fall of 1944, General H. H. Arnold, head of the AAF, personally ordered that 14 planes be made available to carry the atomic bombs as well as to carry instruments in support of the atomic bomb attacks. Another 14 B-29s were to be placed in reserve as replacements for training and operational losses and to meet the emergency needs of the Manhattan Project.

Although some senior AAF officers objected to diverting B-29s from the Pacific bombing campaign, Arnold ordered full and unqualified support for the atomic bomb program. A B-29 Very-Heavy Bomber (VHB) squadron with special units attached was to be assigned to the Manhattan Project as soon as possible. The units

---

THE MANHATTAN PROJECT

Manhattan was the code name for the top-secret U.S. program during World War II to build the atomic bomb. The code name was derived from another code name, the Manhattan Engineer District, a nonexistent region invented by the U.S. Army Corps of Engineers to conceal the atomic bomb enterprise. The Manhattan Project controlled hundreds of millions of dollars' worth of facilities, matériel, and machinery at Oak Ridge, Tennessee; Hanford, Washington; and Los Alamos, New Mexico, plus smaller activities elsewhere.

Of the 300 leading physicists in the United States, about 125 worked on the Manhattan Project. By the summer of 1944 approximately 150,000 civilian scientists and technicians and military personnel were assigned to the research, development, material production, and building of the first bombs.

Major General Leslie R. Groves, an Army engineer, was in overall command of the Manhattan project. (His previous project had been directing construction of the Pentagon building in Washington, D.C.) Groves managed all aspects of the atomic bomb program from its beginnings in 1942 until 1947. The technical director of the Los Alamos laboratory, where the first atomic bombs were designed and built, was Robert J. Oppenheimer.

---

were to be assembled at a base in the southwestern United States for special training, and 14 modified B-29s were to be available by January 1, 1945. U.S. military planners believed that by that time, the war in Europe would be over and that Japan would be the target for the atomic bomb.[9]

Further, any obstruction or delay by AAF officials was to be countered by the single word "Silverplate," which would immediately convey General Arnold's approval. The term would be recognized even by personnel who had absolutely no knowledge of the atomic bomb project. The cover story was planted that Silverplate was a Pullman railroad car to be used by President Roosevelt (given the code name Thin Man) and Prime Minister Winston Churchill (Fat Man) on a secret tour of the United States.

Next, a commanding officer was needed for the bomber unit that would deliver the atomic bomb. General Arnold and his staff selected Lieutenant Colonel Paul W. Tibbets, a veteran of the European and North African air campaigns and one of the most knowledgeable B-29 pilots in the AAF. Tibbets later recalled, "I was given the authority to requisition anything needed to carry out my assignment."[10]

The 393rd Heavy Bombardment Squadron was detached from the 504th Bombardment Group, which was being readied to join the Twentieth Air Force on Tinian. The squadron was selected because of its training record, which included a deployment to Cuba in September 1944 that had provided considerable over-water flying in the Caribbean area. Ten of the squadron's B-29s and 15 crews had deployed to Cuba, flying simulated combat missions with bombing runs from altitudes of 20,000 to 30,000 feet.

The 393rd and other units would form the new 509th Composite Group under Tibbets's command. The term *composite* indicated that the group would be self-sufficient, capable of carrying out its mission without additional support.

Next, an assembly and training base was needed. Wendover Army Air Field was selected. On the Utah-Nevada border, about 100 miles from Salt Lake City, Wendover was isolated and was near the Salton Sea area, where the 509th Composite Group could carry out bombing trials with dummy weapons resembling the atomic bombs in shape. The existing facilities at Wendover, albeit rather primitive, were sufficient for training; hence, no new construction would be needed. Secrecy was the watchword at Wendover, and although the term *atomic bomb* was never used there, the ever-present billboard cautioned

What you hear here
What you see here
When you leave here
Let it stay here!

The component units of the 509th rapidly assembled at Wendover, with the group being formally activated there on December 17, 1944—the 41st anniversary of the Wright Brothers' first flight. Initially the group consisted of:

PAUL W. TIBBETS

Paul Tibbets was pilot of the first aircraft to drop an atomic bomb on Japan. Born in 1915 in Quincy, Illinois, Tibbets entered the Army's air cadet program in 1937. He was a bomber pilot when the United States entered World War II in December 1941. After flying anti-submarine patrols along the east coast of the United States, Tibbets was assigned to fly B-17 Flying Fortress bombers with the Eighth Air Force, based in England.

He flew on the first U.S. air strike against German-occupied Europe, the target being the French city of Rouen. In November 1942, in preparation for the British-American invasion of North Africa, he flew Lieutenant General Dwight D. Eisenhower, the Allied commander, from London to Gibraltar in his B-17.

After flying combat missions in North Africa, he returned to the United States in 1943 to transition to the B-29 Superfortress bomber. He was a military test pilot for the B-29, helped to train the first combat crews, and set up a school for B-29 flight instructors. Tibbets was chosen to command the 509th Composite Group, which would deliver atomic bombs against Japan when that unit was formally activated on December 17, 1944. The following month he was promoted to full colonel. After training at the remote Wendover Field in Utah, the 509th deployed from the United States to Tinian in May–June 1945.

On August 6, 1945, Tibbets piloted the B-29 *Enola Gay* in the atomic bombing of Hiroshima.

After the war Tibbets continued as commander of the 509th, and his planes participated in the Bikini atomic bomb tests in the summer of 1946. Subsequently, Tibbets transitioned to jet-propelled aircraft and held a series of senior positions before retiring from the U.S. Air Force in 1976 with the rank of brigadier general.

Headquarters, 509th Composite Group
Headquarters and Base Services Squadron,
    390th Air Service Group
320th Troop Carrier Squadron
393rd Heavy Bombardment Squadron
603rd Air Engineer Squadron
1027th Air Materiel Squadron
1395th Military Police Company (Aviation)

Subsequently, on March 6, 1945, the 1st Ordnance Squadron (Special) (Aviation) was activated and assigned to the 509th, providing hand-picked machinists, welders, munitions specialists, and other technicians to help with the atomic bomb assembly at an advanced base. By the end of that month, the 509th had about reached its authorized strength of 225 officers and 1,542 enlisted men.[11]

In addition to the B-29s of the 393rd Heavy Bombardment Squadron, the 320th Troop Carrier Squadron—nicknamed the Green Hornets—provided transportation for personnel and high-priority cargo with several four-engine C-54 Skymaster and two-engine C-47 Skytrain transport planes.[12] The 393rd began training with its modified B-29s, especially with breakaway tactics that, after dropping a nuclear weapon, required the aircraft to dive and accelerate to fly as rapidly as possible from the bomb detonation. A distance of eight miles was desired so that the aircraft could withstand the bomb's shock wave.

All B-29s assigned to the 509th had been modified to the Silverplate configuration. The

Colonel Paul W. Tibbets, commanding officer of the 509th Composite Group and pilot of the *Enola Gay* on the Hiroshima mission, shown next to the aircraft sometime after that mission. Before his assignment to the B-29 program, Tibbets flew B-17 Flying Fortresses in the North African and European theaters. (NASM)

initial B-29s given the Silverplate modification were soon being replaced by B-29s with improved engines. One of the latter aircraft was No. 44–86292.

The 15 new Silverplate aircraft had modified forward bomb bays and bomb shackles fitted to carry either of the two atomic bomb designs, the larger Fat Man or the smaller Little Boy (originally called Thin Man). To enhance their performance, the Silverplate aircraft were lightened, with all turrets, guns, fire-control systems, and ammunition removed, except for two .50-caliber machine guns in the tail. The other turret openings were plated over. Special wiring related to release of an atomic bomb was installed and provisions were made for carrying a "special observer." Thus modified, the aircraft were ferried to Wendover, with No. 44–86292 arriving on June 14, 1945.

While scientists and engineers at Los Alamos worked to complete the first atomic bombs, the officers and men of the 509th Composite Group worked to ready their bombers for war.

Meanwhile, the decision was reached to base the 509th Composite Group in the Mariana Islands. The Marianas had been captured in a massive Navy-Marine-Army assault begun in early June 1944 (almost simultaneous with the Allied invasion of Normandy). After savage fighting against Japanese defenders, the island of Saipan, the northernmost of the major islands in the Marianas, was declared secure by U.S. forces on July 9. The second major island selected for airfields was Tinian, south of

Saipan; it was declared secure from Japanese troops on August 12.[13] Immediately after the capture of Saipan and Tinian, U.S. Army and Navy engineers began constructing massive bomber airfields on the islands for B-29s. Two were built on Tinian, Isley Field and North Field, as was a major port. On March 30, 1945, Colonel Elmer E. Kirkpatrick of the Manhattan Project's staff arrived in the Marianas to talk with Admiral Chester W. Nimitz, Commander-in-Chief of Pacific Ocean Areas, and Major General Curtis LeMay, commander, XXI Bomber Command. Both Nimitz and LeMay had their headquarters on the island of Guam. Kirkpatrick had been sent to choose a base for the 509th Composite Group.

This was probably the first that General LeMay had heard about the atomic bomb. Nimitz had been informed earlier, in February 1945, because the Marianas were within his command area and he had questioned the plans to send the "nonstandard" 509th Composite Group into his theater.[14]

General LeMay flew Kirkpatrick to nearby Tinian, where they selected the North Field as base for the 509th. Tinian, which is 12 miles long and 6 miles at its widest point, is 1,450 miles from Tokyo. A Navy construction battalion—the Seabees—was assigned to build the facilities for the group.

The massive buildup in the Marianas, both as a base for B-29 strikes against Japan and as a forward base for future amphibious assaults, led to a massive shipping jam as many hundreds of merchant ships reached the Marianas. Scores of cargo ships waited offshore to unload, with priority given to shipments of fuel and conventional bombs for the ongoing bombing of Japan. Admiral Nimitz directed that the 509th's facilities be prepared at the utmost speed and that ships carrying material for the 509th should have priority in unloading their cargo.

The most significant of the 509th facilities on Tinian would be the bomb-component storage and assembly buildings and the bomb-loading pit. The low clearance between the open B-29

bomb bay doors and the ground, coupled with the large size of the Fat Man bomb, necessitated that a pit be constructed. The B-29 would be towed over the pit and then a hydraulic lift would raise the bomb into the bay, where it could be attached to the special shackles. Also, an atomic bomb loading facility was to be built on Iwo Jima, which had been assaulted by U.S. troops on February 19, 1945. If the bomb-carrying plane encountered problems after takeoff from Tinian, it was to try to land on Iwo Jima, halfway between Tinian and Japan. The bomb would then be unloaded from the original plane and transferred to another Silverplate B-29, which would be standing by on Iwo Jima in the event of such an emergency.

In late April the first elements of the 509th began shipping out. Major support units boarded trains for Fort Lawton, Washington, and the nearby Seattle port of embarkation. The lead elements embarked in the merchant ship *Cape Victory*, which departed Seattle on May 6, bound for Honolulu, Eniwetok, and Tinian, a 23-day voyage. The advanced echelon of the 509th departed Wendover by air beginning the morning of May 15. Three of the C-54s from the Green Hornet squadron carried 29 officers and 61 enlisted men to Tinian, with brief stopovers at Oahu, Johnston Island, and Kwajalein. The first C-54 reached Tinian early on the morning of May 18. (A total of some 520 men of the 509th were flown to Tinian; the remainder—more than 1,000 men—and almost all of their equipment went by ship.)

The group's B-29s began departing Wendover for their base on Tinian on June 5, with the first three aircraft arriving on June 11. Eleven aircraft were at Tinian by the end of June, and four additional planes arrived in early July. No. 44–86292 was one of the last Silverplate B-29s to reach Tinian, having left Wendover on June 27 and touched down at North Field on July 6.

The 509th Composite Group was ready for combat by early July, albeit not yet for nuclear strikes.

B-29S OF THE 509TH COMPOSITE GROUP

AAF records differ as to whether the group had 15, 17, or 18 aircraft on Tinian in the Mariana Islands. Fifteen was the most likely number. Group records for early August 1945 list 15 aircraft. The side numbers are those assigned by the group.

Side number	AAF serial	Name
71	44–27303	*Jabbitt III*
72	44–27302	*Top Secret*
73	44–27300	*Strange Cargo*
77	44–27297	*Bockscar*
82	44–86292	*Enola Gay*
83	44–27298	*Full House*
84	44–27296	[none]
85	44–27301	*Straight Flush*
86	44–27299	*Next Objective*
88	44–27304	*Up An' Atom*
89	44–27353	*The Great Artiste*
90	44–27354	[none]
91	44–27291	*Necessary Evil*
94	44–27346	[none]
95	44–86347	*Laggin' Dragon*

It is believed that all of the aircraft had been named before August 6, 1945, except for the *Necessary Evil* and *Up An' Atom*, which were named after the first atomic strike. *Bockscar* was actually "Bock's Car," named for pilot Frederick Bock, but the aircraft's name should be used as it was actually painted on the fuselage.

The *Enola Gay* is preserved at the National Air and Space Museum, on display at the museum's Dulles Airport facility outside of Washington, D.C. The *Bockscar* is on display at the Air Force Museum at Wright-Patterson AFB outside of Dayton, Ohio.

THE MISSION

3

As the officers and enlisted men of the 509th Composite Group settled into their tents and Quonset huts at North Field on Tinian, Colonel Paul Tibbets began an intense training program for his B-29 flight crews and his group staff. North Field had four parallel runways, each 8,500 feet long, reputed to be the longest operational runways then in existence.

Parking spots for the hundreds of B-29s of several bombardment wings surrounded the runways. There were massive fuel and ammunition depots, maintenance areas, and tent cities and hundreds of Quonset huts for flight and ground crews who supported those bombers as they took off almost daily on their long flights to strike the Japanese home islands.[1] More B-29 runways were located farther south on the island at Isley Field.

Upon arrival all flight crews were required to attend a ground school. The seven-day course consisted of bailout, ditching, life-raft drill, and rescue procedures; survival skills; radar-bombing techniques; area weather considerations; information on the Japanese people; and wing and command regulations. (For administration the 509th was assigned to the 313th Bomb Wing at North Field.)

The arrival of the 509th bombers on Tinian and the distinctive arrowhead within a circle on their large tail fins soon came to the attention of the Japanese.[2] Radio Tokyo's chief propagandist—Tokyo Rose—called attention to the group almost as soon as their B-29s landed on Tinian. The few remaining Japanese troops in hiding on the island were able to communicate the arrival of U.S. bomber units on Tinian to Japan by radio.

The 509th began training flights from Tinian on June 30. The first long-range, over-water bombing mission came on July 1 when nine B-29s flew north to Iwo Jima, then returned to Rota, a small island in the Marianas still held by the Japanese, and released their bombs. The aircraft used so-called Pumpkin bombs, which simulated the size and shape of the Fat Man atomic bomb. There was no anti-aircraft fire from the beleaguered defenders of Rota. Aircraft No. 44–86292 made the first of those training flights from Tinian on July 12. The plane's pilot and aircraft commander was Captain Robert A. Lewis, who had flown the plane from Wendover to Tinian. Some of the Pumpkin bombings against Rota and other islands in the area were undertaken to test various components of the actual atomic bombs. Based in part on those operations, modifications were made to the atomic bombs both at Los Alamos and on Tinian almost up to the eve of the their being loaded into the B-29s that would carry them to Japan.

PUMPKIN BOMBS

"Pumpkin" was the name given to stand-in bombs for the atomic bombs. The Pumpkin bombs were used to provide B-29 Super-fortress crews with experience in aiming and releasing the unique shape of the Fat Man. The Pumpkins were fashioned by the Manhattan Project, and some were painted orange for visibility during test drops.

Early Pumpkins simulated the shape and weight of the Fat Man bomb. Subsequently, the 509th Composite Group dropped Pumpkins containing 5,500 pounds of high explosives (black powder or TORPEX) with a proximity fuse that allowed an air burst, a feature of the atomic bomb.

The first true combat mission of the 509th was against Marcus Island, a bypassed Japanese holding northeast of Tinian, about the same distance away as Iwo Jima. There was some anti-aircraft fire, but no enemy fighters were encountered. Marcus became a regular target for the 509th bombers. Captain Lewis and his crew made their first bombing strike against Marcus on July 21. Of those strikes, Tibbets remembered

To other outfits on Tinian, we were a bunch of pampered dandies. While they were flying hazardous bombing missions, from which some did not return, our crews were making training flights with an occasional sortie into the enemy skies to drop a single bomb from high altitude.[3]

After several weeks of routine training flights and almost 40 bombing missions with conventional and Pumpkin bombs against

nearby islands and Marcus, Tibbets ordered the group to begin Pumpkin-bombing strikes of selected targets in Japan. The Pumpkin missions would familiarize aircrews with over-water navigation to reach the Japanese home islands and give them lessons in target recognition. It was also hoped that the missions would lull Japanese air defense officials into not reacting strongly to flights of only three B-29s over Japan with one releasing a single bomb.

Each three-plane bombing formation would consist of the bomb-carrying plane, one with instruments to monitor the atom bomb's detonation, and a camera-carrying aircraft. Working with the Twentieth Air Force's planning staff, Tibbets selected specific military targets for the Pumpkin bombs. Like the other B-29s that were striking the Japanese home islands, Tibbets's planes were to avoid cities that had been placed on a reserved list for possible strikes with atomic bombs.

The potential atomic bomb targets were initially selected by the Target Committee in Washington, which consisted of military officers and civilians, including three from General Arnold's staff in Washington, four from the Manhattan Project, and a member of the British team at the Los Alamos laboratory, in addition to others with knowledge of the atomic bomb. Their criteria for targets included that they contain important military or industrial installations, be within range of a loaded B-29 flying from Tinian, and be suitable for visual bombing, as opposed to locating the specific aim point by radar.[4] Major General Leslie Groves wanted visual bombing of the target cities. Considered more accurate than radar bombing, the accuracy of visual bombing was important to enable Manhattan Project's scientists to estimate the distance of different levels of damage from the aim point.

General Groves wanted to test the bomb's effectiveness by striking Japanese cities that had suffered little or no damage from conventional Army Air Forces (AAF) and Navy bombings. Secretary of War Henry Stimson and General Arnold developed a list of potential target cities for the atomic bomb. None was to be attacked by other forces. Thus, four Japanese cities were selected as potential atomic bomb targets in order of priority for attack: Hiroshima, Kokura, Niigata, and Nagasaki. All of the target cities were major military ports or had major military and industrial facilities located in them. The city of Kyoto was initially considered, but because it was a national shrine of religion and culture, that city was withdrawn from the target list and the city of Nagasaki was added in its place.[5] Tokyo was never considered as a target for the atomic bomb, in part because it had been largely destroyed in a massive firebombing in March 1945, because it contained few military targets, and because the Emperor and his family resided in Tokyo's Imperial Palace.

The first conventional bombing attack by the 509th Composite Group against the Japanese home islands began at 2 A.M. on July 20 when the first of the group's B-29s lifted from the long runways of North Field. Ten aircraft took off to strike four different cities. For these strikes each plane—including No. 44–86292—carried a single Pumpkin bomb. Five of the planes bombed their primary targets, although clouds forced two of them to use radar to release their bombs. Four others dropped their bombs on secondary targets using radar, and the tenth B-29 was forced to jettison its bomb at sea en route to Japan because of an engine failure.

The results of the mission were recorded as "fair to unobserved." A disappointing performance for the massive effort expended to get those ten B-29s over Japan. An unapproved incident occurred during this Pumpkin strike: One B-29 pilot, Major Claude Eatherly, found his assigned target near Tokyo obscured by clouds. He then decided to drop his Pumpkin bomb on the Imperial Palace, a target prohibited to all American bombers. The weather over Tokyo also was unfavorable, and none of the crew knew the precise location of the palace. The bomb was released over the city, but missed the palace.[6] (Upon returning to Tinian, Eatherly was chewed out by Tibbets, but remained an aircraft commander.)

A few hours later, Radio Tokyo commented on the 509th bombing attacks:

The tactics of the raiding enemy planes have become so complicated that they cannot be anticipated from experience or the common sense gained so far. The single B-29 which passed over the capital this morning dropping bombs [sic] on one section of the Tokyo Metropolis, taking unawares slightly the people of the city, and these are certainly so-called sneak tactics aimed at confusing [the minds of the people].[7]

A second ten-plane strike mission was flown by the 509th on July 24, attacking three Japanese cities. Nine planes bombed visually, one by radar. This time the intelligence assessment was that the mission was "effective and successful."

Two more Pumpkin strikes were flown over Japan during the month, with ten B-29s on July 26 against two cities and with eight aircraft on July 29 against three cities.[8] In four strikes against Japan, the B-29s had released 37 Pumpkin bombs. The only combat damaged suffered by the aircraft was minor damage to one B-29, probably from anti-aircraft fire. Japanese fighters were sighted, but they made no attempts to attack the bombers. Tibbets did not fly on those missions; he knew more about the atomic bomb project than any other officer in the AAF and was forbidden from flying missions that could expose him to capture by the Japanese.

As hoped for, Japanese air defenses did not overreact to the 509th bombing missions. Few Japanese fighters rose to intercept the B-29s while their bombing altitude of 30,000 feet generally made them immune to anti-aircraft fire.

Meanwhile, preparations were underway for the atomic bombing of Japan. Tibbets briefed six of his B-29 crews on the special procedures for handling and dropping the atomic bombs. Using reconnaissance photos, Tibbets, his lead bombardier, Major Thomas W.

(Tom) Ferebee, his lead navigator, Captain Theodore J. (Dutch) Van Kirk, and William G. Penney of the British mission to the project, began selecting aim points in the target cities. Selections were based on navigation considerations, the ease of finding the aim points visually, and the desire to obtain maximum damage from the bomb.

On July 29 a B-29 flew a dummy Little Boy atomic bomb to Iwo Jima, where the plane taxied over the loading pit. The dummy bomb was unloaded and then reloaded back into the same B-29 in a test of the backup plan should the original bomber have to abort the mission and the bomb have to be shifted to an alternate Silverplate B-29. On July 31 the bomb shape was again flown to Iwo Jima, unloaded, and reloaded into a second B-29 and flown back to Tinian. As the second B-29 flew off Tinian, the shape was released into the sea, the drop being observed by Manhattan Project officials on the island.

To undertake the final assembly and preparation of the atomic bombs on Tinian, General Groves had dispatched a team of 37 scientists and engineers to work with the 1st Ordnance Squadron (Special) (Aviation). The team from Los Alamos consisted of 7 Navy officers, 1 Army officer, 17 Army enlisted men, and 12 civilians, the last wearing Army uniforms with appropriate Army rank—the presence of civilians on the bomber base would have caused too many questions. All were under the command of Navy captain William S. Parsons. Their effort to prepare the atomic bombs was code-named Alberta.

The first atomic bomb—a Fat Man–type device—had been successfully detonated atop a 103-foot steel tower at Alamogordo in the New Mexico wilderness on July 16, 1945. Called Trinity, the test demonstrated the feasibility of an implosion-type (plutonium) bomb. It detonated in a blinding explosion equivalent in force to 18,600 tons of TNT (i.e., 18.6 kilotons). There was no need to test the Little Boy gun-type (uranium) bomb because its detonation principal was much simpler than that of an implosion bomb.

USING THE BOMB IN COMBAT

At the time of the Alamogordo test, President Harry S. Truman was meeting in the Berlin suburb of Potsdam with Prime Minister Winston Churchill and Soviet premier Josef Stalin. On July 26 American radio stations beamed to Tokyo the so-called Potsdam Proclamation, whose words, Truman hoped, would end the war; it began, "We—the President of the United States, the President of the National Government of the Republic of China, and the Prime Minister of Great Britain—representing the hundreds of millions of our countrymen, have conferred and agree that Japan shall be given an opportunity to end this war." (Stalin was excluded from the announcement because the Soviet Union was not then at war with Japan.) The proclamation—President Truman called it "our ultimatum"—warned that unless Japan surrendered, Allied military forces were "poised to strike the final blows upon Japan." The Japanese government quickly rejected the proclamation.

President Harry S. Truman personally made the decision to employ atomic bombs against Japan after learning of the successful Trinity test of an atomic bomb on July 16, 1945. At the time he was meeting in the Berlin suburb of Potsdam with British prime minister Winston Churchill (left) and Soviet leader Josef Stalin (right). (U.S. Navy)

On July 25, Lieutenant General Carl A. Spaatz, commander of the U.S. Strategic Air Forces in the Pacific, received—via General Groves in Washington—an order from the acting Chief of Staff of the Army, General Thomas T. Handy, authorizing the 509th Composite Group to "deliver its first special bomb as soon as weather will permit visual bombing after about 3 August 1945 on one of the targets: Hiroshima, Kokura, Niigata and Nagasaki." The order continued, "Additional bombs will be delivered on the above targets as soon as made ready."[9] President Truman knew of the order. In response to a July 30 message from Washington asking for approval to employ the atomic bombs, Truman scrawled a note that said, "Release when ready but not sooner than August 2."[10] (President Truman did not want the first bomb dropped until he had departed from Potsdam.)

Components of both types of bombs were being flown to Tinian, both in B-29s and in C-54s, including those operated by the 509th's Green Hornet transport squadron. The heavy U235 components for the Little Boy bomb were transported by truck from Los Alamos to nearby Kirkland Air Force Base (AFB), then by plane to San Francisco, where they were taken to the Hunter's Point Navy Yard and loaded on the cruiser *Indianapolis*. The ship, with two Army officers from Los Alamos on board to escort and monitor the special cargo, sailed on July 16 and sped to Oahu and then on to Tinian, arriving on July 26. Her secret cargo was unloaded the same day, and the ship sailed for a brief stopover at Guam, then set course for the Philippines. (Her transit ended shortly after midnight on July 30 when she was torpedoed by a Japanese submarine some 600 miles southwest of Guam; of her crew of 1,199, only 317 men survived the sinking and several days in shark-infested waters.[11])

The atomic bomb assembly team on Tinian completed assembling the Little Boy (known as bomb L-11) on July 31. The first atomic bomb was thus ready for use on August 1. President Truman's order meant that it could be used anytime after August 2.

But predicted weather conditions over Japan delayed the mission until August 6. During the bomb's preparation, there were discussions about the danger of the bomb-carrying aircraft's crashing on takeoff. Several heavily laden B-29s had crashed while taking off from airfields on both Saipan and Tinian. Serious consideration was given to evacuating the nearly 20,000 people from Tinian before the start of the strike mission. This would have been a ponderous, difficult, time-consuming operation, and the idea was abandoned as unfeasible and unnecessary.[12]

LITTLE BOY ATOMIC BOMB

The Little Boy was the first atomic bomb used in combat. Developed by the Manhattan Project, it differed from the Fat Man atomic bomb by using the gun principle for attaining the critical mass necessary for creating a supercritical mass of uranium$_{235}$.

The Little Boy was 10½ feet long, 29 inches in diameter, and weighed 9,700 pounds. The steel gun barrel of the weapon was approximately six feet long and weighed about 1,000 pounds. A uranium projectile was fired electrically through the barrel, propelled by several pounds of cordite. Projectile velocity reached 1,000 feet per second and was driven into a uranium tube in the front of the bomb to form the supercritical mass necessary for a nuclear detonation.

There was no preoperational test of the Little Boy as there was of the Fat Man because of the simplicity of the design and the scarcity of the critical nuclear material. The Little Boy dropped on Hiroshima had a yield of approximately 15 kilotons.

In addition to the Hiroshima bomb, five additional Little Boy weapon assemblies were produced between August 1945 and February 1950. That atomic bomb model was in the U.S. nuclear inventory until January 1951.

At an early stage of the atomic bomb project, the Little Boy was known as the Thin Man.

The Little Boy atomic bomb dropped on Hiroshima shortly after it was assembled on Tinian on August 5, 1945. The bomb was placed on a dolly for transportation to the pit from which it could be raised up into the *Enola Gay*'s forward bomb bay. These bomb-loading photos are taken from a U.S. Army film. (From AAF/Los Alamos National Laboratory film)

would fly on the first atomic bomb mission as the weapons officer, decided that he would insert the plugs by hand after the bomber was airborne. By that time Colonel Tibbets had selected aircraft No. 44–86292 to deliver the Little Boy bomb. Accordingly, a small folding platform was built in the forward bomb bay of the aircraft. After the B-29 was airborne, but before it reached an altitude that required pressurization, Parsons and his assistant, Army 2nd Lieutenant Morris R. Jeppson of the 1st Ordnance Squadron, would climb onto the platform and arm the weapon.

On the morning of August 5, the weather forecasters predicted suitable weather over the Japanese home islands for a visual bombing attack the following day. That day Major General Curtis LeMay, the senior B-29 commander in the Marianas, issued Special Bomb Operational Order No. 13 to the 509th Composite Group to carry out the first nuclear attack. The primary target was to be

Conventional bombs were armed before the B-29s took off, and the intention was to do the same with the atomic bombs; however, a two-piece breech plug had to be inserted into the Little Boy bomb to arm the weapon. The larger piece was an outer, ring-shaped plug that screwed into threads in the breech end of the gun tube. A smaller, inner plug that contained the primers and firing leads for igniting the propellant screwed into the threads in the center of the outer plug. The inner plug, which was about three inches in diameter, could be inserted by hand.[13]

After coded radio discussions with Los Alamos, Captain "Deak" Parsons, who

The Little Boy atomic bomb. (AAF)

Hiroshima, with Kokura and Nagasaki named as alternate targets in the event that Hiroshima was obscured by clouds or there was some other last-minute reason not to bomb the target.

That day Tibbets had his mother's maiden name—*Enola Gay*—painted on the nose of aircraft No. 44–86292. The aircraft was towed to the loading pit, and with scores of heavily armed military policemen standing guard, the Little Boy was lifted into the forward bomb bay and secured to the bomb shackles. Shortly after noon the loading procedure was completed.

Captain Parsons and Lieutenant Jeppson then entered the *Enola Gay*'s bomb bay and spent about two hours practicing the plug insertion procedures. Parsons was confident that he could arm the bomb while in flight. The bomb bay doors were closed, and a heavy guard was posted around the area. Tibbets then had the tail insignia of the 509th Composite Group removed from the *Enola Gay* and the six other aircraft that would participate in the strike. Instead of the encircled arrowhead, the aircraft were given the circle-R insignia of 6th Bombardment Group. Reportedly, Tokyo Rose broadcasted the insignia change a few hours afterwards![14]

Finally, the radio call sign of the bomb-carrying aircraft was changed from the 509th's "Victor" to "Dimples." The *Enola Gay*, with side number 82, would be known as "Dimples 82" in radio communications.

Also on August 5 several members of the atomic bomb loading team were flown to Iwo Jima to be ready to shift the atomic

The Little Boy in the loading pit at North Field on Tinian. A similar pit was prepared on Iwo Jima, about halfway to Japan, in the event that an atom bomb–carrying B-29 encountered mechanical or other problems and the bomb had to be transferred to another Silverplate-configured B-29. (From AAF/Los Alamos National Laboratory film)

The Little Boy about to be loaded up into the forward bomb bay of the *Enola Gay*. The aircraft's radar dome—located between the bomb bays—is visible beyond the bomb. The atomic bombs were too large to load into the aircraft without the use of the pits, which were fitted with a hydraulic bomb lift. (From AAF/Los Alamos National Laboratory film)

The Little Boy being raised up into the *Enola Gay*. The Silverplate-configured aircraft had pneumatically operated bomb bay doors, which could open and close much faster than the electrically operated bomb doors of standard B-29s. (From AAF/Los Alamos National Laboratory film)

bomb to another B-29 in the event of an emergency that forced the *Enola Gay* to land on that island before releasing the bomb over Japan. There, too, heavy security precautions were put into effect.

At 11 P.M. special briefings were held for the crews of the three aircraft of the strike group—the *Enola Gay*, *The Great Artiste*, which would carry observers and instruments, and No. 91 (later named *Necessary Evil*), which would serve as the photo plane on the mission.[15] The accompanying planes would be piloted by Major Charles Sweeney, commander of the 393rd Heavy Bombardment Squadron, and Captain George Marquardt, respectively.[16] In addition to their crews, the two accompanying planes would carry observers from the Manhattan Project.

Colonel Tibbets, Captain Parsons, and Dr. Norman Ramsey of the Manhattan Project briefed the crews, telling them of the estimated power of the Little Boy and the probable damage to the target. Captain Parsons began his comments by saying, "The bomb you are going to drop is something new in the history of warfare. It is the most destructive weapon ever produced. We think it will knock out everything within a three mile area."[17]

About midnight breakfast was served to the crews and observers who would man the seven planes participating in the first atomic bombing. Their menu: real eggs (instead of the usual reconstituted powdered eggs normally served on Tinian), sausage, rolled oats, and apple butter, with milk or coffee to drink. Shortly after 1:30 A.M. on August 6, the three weather-reporting planes from the 509th took off—*Full House*, *Jabbitt III*, and *Straight Flush*. Each of those B-29s would streak northward and report weather conditions over the three target cities.

The crews for the three other B-29s that would participate in the Hiroshima mission arrived at their planes at 1:40 A.M., laden with flight and survival gear—bulletproof flight vests, .45-caliber pistols, parachutes, life jackets, and box lunches for their 13-hour flight. The *Enola Gay* carried several items never before carried by B-29s flying to Japan. Inside of the plane's forward bomb bay was the Little Boy atomic bomb. And, in his coveralls pocket, Colonel Tibbets had a container of 11 cyanide tablets, one for each member of the crew. He had already given one tablet to Captain Parsons. U.S. officials were aware that B-29 crewmen were being tortured and executed by the Japanese. Tibbets and Parsons, of course, had extensive knowledge of the atomic bomb program, which had the potential to make them especially vulnerable to torture.

It was unknown how Colonel Tibbets would distribute the tablets to the crew, especially to the tail gunner who was isolated from the rest of the plane when it was pressurized. Indeed, even an in-flight emergency or battle damage could make the distribution impractical, if not impossible.

General Groves had wanted the takeoff recorded, and floodlights illuminated the *Enola Gay* while movie cameras whirred. The crewmen climbed aboard; Lewis, the plane's pilot and aircraft commander, would sit in the right-hand seat for this flight. With Tibbets in the pilot's seat, the flight crew consisted of

Radar countermeasures	1st Lieutenant Jacob Beser, USA
Tail gunner	Staff Sergeant George R. Caron, USA
Flight engineer	Technical Sergeant Wyatt E. Duzenbury, USA
Bombardier	Major Thomas W. Ferebee, USA
Copilot	Captain Robert A. Lewis, USA
Radio operator	Private First Class Richard H. Nelson, USA
Assistant engineer	Sergeant Robert H. Shumard, USA
Radar operator	Sergeant Joseph S. Stiborik, USA
Pilot/aircraft commander	Colonel Paul W. Tibbets, USA
Navigator	Captain Theodore J. Van Kirk, USA

Shortly before the *Enola Gay* took off for Hiroshima, the 509th Composite Group's ground maintenance officer, Lieutenant Colonel John Porter, posed with the flight crew: standing, from left: Porter, Theodore J. Van Kirk, Thomas W. Ferebee, Paul W. Tibbets, Robert A. Lewis, and Jacob Beser; kneeling: Joseph S. Stiborik, George R. Caron, Richard H. Nelson, Robert H. Shumard, Wyatt E. Duzenbury. Not present were Navy Captain William Parsons and Lieutenant Morris Jeppson, who also flew on the Hiroshima mission. (AAF/NASM)

Then, at 2:45 A.M. on August 6, the *Enola Gay* rolled down the runway, and the heavily laden aircraft took off without difficulty. It was followed at two-minute intervals by *The Great Artiste* and No. 91 in the strike group, plus the B-29 that would land on Iwo Jima and stand by for an emergency bomb transfer. Each plane took off from one of the four parallel runways of North Field.

The flight northward was uneventful. In the *Enola Gay*, eight minutes after takeoff, Parsons and Jeppson climbed down into the forward bomb bay to arm Little Boy as they had practiced on Tinian. Jeppson held a flashlight in the freezing bomb bay while Parsons worked. The operation was completed in 15 minutes.

The *Enola Gay* sighted Iwo Jima—halfway to the target—at 5:55 A.M. The *Top Secret* landed on the island, while the two other planes formed a formation on the *Enola Gay*, and at 6:07 A.M. they continued northward toward Japan. At 7:41 A.M., the *Enola Gay* climbed to the intended bombing altitude of 32,700 feet. A half-hour later Major Eatherly, piloting the *Straight Flush*, radioed a coded message to Tibbets that weather conditions over the primary target were suitable for visual bombing. The other weather planes reported that the skies were also clear over Nagasaki, but that a ground haze obscured Kokura. There were no other U.S. planes near the target cities. All were for-

Captain Parsons and Lieutenant Jeppson brought the number of men on board the *Enola Gay* to 12. The engines started up without trouble. When he was ready to start taxiing, Tibbets leaned out of the cockpit window and tried to wave the bystanders away. Someone yelled "wave" to him, and he gave a well-photographed friendly wave to the camera.

bidden to approach within 50 miles for four hours before and six hours after the planned attack.

Tibbets discussed the situation with Parsons, and they agreed that they would attack Hiroshima. Located on the southern side of the main island of Honshu, Hiroshima was a major port, the transshipment point for troops and equipment being sent to the southern island of Kyushu, and a target of the U.S. amphibious assault planned for November 1945. Hiroshima also was headquarters for a major Army command and contained several significant defense factories. It was counted as Japan's eighth largest city, although it had shrunk from a population of 365,000 in 1943 to 245,000 at the time of the attack.

As the *Enola Gay* approached the aim point, the aircraft was at 31,600 feet traveling at 328 mph ground speed. Tibbets, Van Kirk, and Parsons confirmed the aim point, a T-shaped bridge in the center of the city. Ferebee sighted the aim point through the Norden bombsight, and Tibbets switched control of the plane to the automatic bombing system.

At 9:14:17 A.M. Ferebee switched on the high-pitched audio tone that would sound for 60 seconds.[18] The tone was broadcast to the two accompanying B-29s, as well as the three weather planes, which were already en route back to Tinian. When the tone stopped the bomb bay doors opened automatically, and the Little Boy was released. Simultaneously, the bomb bay doors opened on *The Great Artiste* and three blast gauge packages were released to be monitored by scientists in the aircraft as they fell toward the ground.

The instant that the *Enola Gay*'s bomb bay doors were closed Colonel Tibbets placed the aircraft into a step dive to the right, accelerating to escape the blast. The bomb fell for 45.5 seconds and detonated at an altitude of 1,900 feet above Hiroshima.[19]

An instant later Hiroshima was devastated.

Colonel Tibbets estimated that the *Enola Gay* was about 15 miles "slant range" from the explosion when the shock wave struck the plane. The *Enola Gay* and nearby *The Great Artiste* suffered severe jolts, but neither plane was damaged. When the planes turned back toward Hiroshima the mushroom-shaped cloud was already at 30,000 feet and rising rapidly. After circling the cloud, the planes set course for Tinian. Parsons radioed the results of the attack to Iwo Jima, which relayed it to Tinian, which sent word of the successful attack on to General Groves in Washington.

The mushroom cloud still could be seen from the *Enola Gay* when it was 360 miles from Hiroshima at an altitude of 26,000 feet. Four hours after the attack, two camera-equipped B-29s (designated F-13s) tried to photograph the target, but clouds and smoke obscured their view. They reported fires still raging below.

Beneath those flames Hiroshima was demolished. The bomb's force was equivalent to 15,000 tons of TNT. At least 140,000 people were killed or would die from radiation or other injuries by the end of the year.[20]

The return flight of the strike group was uneventful, except for a lone Japanese fighter that approached the B-29s, but did not attack.[21] The *Enola Gay* landed safely at North Field on Tinian at 2:58 P.M., followed a few minutes later by *The Great Artiste* and No. 91. The *Enola Gay* had been airborne for 12 hours, 13 minutes.

As Tibbets taxied the plane to its parking space, several hundred people were waiting—the senior AAF officers from the Marianas and hundreds of men from the 509th, plus a mass of photographers. Tibbets was the first to climb down from the plane. He was immediately congratulated and presented with the Distinguished Service Cross. A formal debriefing was conducted by the group intelligence officer, while the crews sipped lemonade and bourbon.

At the time of the Hiroshima bombing, President Truman was on board the heavy cruiser *Augusta* in the North Atlantic, returning to the United States from the meeting of Allied leaders in Potsdam. Sixteen hours after the attack, while he was eating lunch with members of the crew of the *Augusta*, Captain Frank

The aim point for the Little Boy at Hiroshima was the T-bridge. The bridge survived the atomic blast, but, as shown in this photo taken on October 6, 1945, most of the city was devastated. A few concrete buildings survived, although they were wrecked. (AAF/NASM)

The *Enola Gay* landing at Tinian on the afternoon of August 6 after the Hiroshima mission. The *Enola Gay*'s mission was flawless, compared with the problem-plagued flight of *Bockscar* on the Nagasaki mission three days later. (AAF/NASM)

The now-familiar atomic cloud billows skyward over Hiroshima shortly after the Little Boy detonation at 9:15 A.M. on August 6, 1945. At the time this photo was taken, the atomic cloud had reached 20,000 feet. (AAF)

Graham, the President's watch officer, entered the mess and handed the President a radio message from the Secretary of War: "Big Bomb dropped on Hiroshima August 5 at 7:15 P.M. Washington time. First reports indicate complete success which was even more conspicuous than earlier test."[22]

While Truman told applauding *Augusta* sailors about "the dropping of a powerful new bomb," in Washington the White House released a statement to the press describing the bomb as "more than 2,000 times the blast power of the British 'grand slam' which was the largest bomb ever yet used in the history of warfare." It said that the effort to produce the bomb was "the greatest achievement of organized science in history." Then, the statement, although aimed at an American audience, spoke directly to the Japanese people:

It was to spare the Japanese people from utter destruction that the ultimatum of July 26 was issued at Potsdam. Their leaders promptly rejected that ultimatum. If they do not now accept our terms, they may expect a rain of ruin from the air, the like of which has never been seen on this earth.[23]

That night, on Tinian, the Manhattan Project technicians and 1st Ordnance Squadron personnel completed their checks on the Fat Man bomb (designated F-31). Ground crews readied their group's B-29s for a second nuclear strike.

The *Enola Gay* taxing at North Field on Tinian moments after landing on August 6. The B-29 flights to Japan and back were exhausting for the men and aircraft based in the Marianas. AAF airfields on Guam, Tinian, and Okinawa were designated North Field. (AAF)

The following day each crew member of the three planes that participated in the Hiroshima strike and their ground crews were awarded the Silver Star medal. Parsons was promoted to the rank of commodore (the equivalent of brigadier general).

THE SECOND ATOMIC STRIKE

The original date scheduled for the second atomic strike against Japan was August 11. Weather predictions indicated a storm would be over the target areas on that date, and the attack was tentatively planned for August 9. Meanwhile, on August 8 the 509th sent six B-29s against two Japanese cities with Pumpkin bombs. The *Enola Gay* returned to Japan on those strikes, piloted this time by Captain Lewis. One of the 509th B-29s was forced to abort and return to Tinian, landing safely with its Pumpkin bomb on board. At the same time conventional bombing attacks by B-29s from the Marianas and Okinawa continued against targets in Japan.

The Fat Man bomb was loaded into *Bockscar* on the morning of August 8 amidst heavy security measures. Later that day Major Charles Sweeney dropped a dummy Fat Man off Tinian from the B-29 *The Great Artiste* in a final practice flight.

The second atomic bomb strike was launched from North Field early on August 9. Shortly before the crews boarded their B-29s on

A specialist "paints" the Fat Man atomic bomb after the batteries and fuses have been installed in the weapon. Assembly of the bomb had begun on August 7, with the initial placement of the high-explosive blocks that would create the implosion to detonate the weapon. (From AAF/Los Alamos National Laboratory film)

The Fat Man atomic bomb being rolled out of the assembly facility at North Field on Tinian. Note the very different shape of this implosion weapon compared with the Little Boy gun weapon. They were also known as plutonium and uranium weapons, respectively. (AAF)

the morning of August 9, the *Bockscar*'s ground crew found that a fuel pump, used to transfer fuel, was inoperable, meaning that 600 gallons of fuel in the rear bomb bay tank could not be used.[24] After a hurried discussion, the decision was made to proceed with the mission. It would have required at least four hours to reload the bomb into another plane. The unusable fuel in *Bockscar*—weighing 3,600 pounds—could not be drained and would have to be carried to Japan and back.

Major Sweeney led the attack in the bomb-carrying B-29 *Bockscar*.[25] Aboard *Bockscar* was Navy Commander Frederick L. Ashworth, assigned to the Manhattan Project, who would serve as weapons officer on the flight, with 1st Lieutenant Philip Barnes of the 1st Ordnance Squadron as his assistant. Also in the *Bockscar*

Again, a special bomb trailer was used to move the Fat Man bomb to the loading pit, a 20-minute trip with the trailer being towed by a large truck at about four miles per hour. At the pit the trailer containing the bomb was placed over the hydraulic lift and lowered into the pit. (From AAF/Los Alamos National Laboratory film)

The B-29 *Bockscar* backing over the bomb pit on the afternoon of August 8. The assembly, movement, and loading of both atomic bombs on Tinian went smoothly through the efforts of military and civilian technicians (the latter wearing Army uniforms) from the Manhattan Project and the Army's 1st Ordnance Squadron (Special) (Aviation). (From AAF/Los Alamos National Laboratory film)

The Fat Man bomb being raised up into forward bomb bay of *Bockscar*. The loading was completed by 8 P.M. on August 8. The bomber was then towed to its hardstand and placed under heavy guard until the early morning takeoff on August 9. Members of the atomic bomb technical teams also stood watch on their charges after they were loaded. (From AAF/Los Alamos National Laboratory film)

was 1st Lieutenant Jacob Beser, radar countermeasures officer. He was the only man to fly on both of the atomic bomb missions.

Beser's job, in his own words, was "to 'baby sit' the electronic proximity fuse in the [atomic bomb] and to be absolutely certain that no signals were present that could inadvertently or prematurely cause the bomb to explode, or even jam the fuse such that it would fail to function."[26] Thus, Beser monitored several black boxes in the B-29 that could detect Japanese electronic signals that might interfere with the bomb's radar fuse (intended to detonate the bomb at a specified distance above the ground).

The bombs had four separate air-burst fuses. Beser explained,

> We had the option of switching off one, two, or even all four of the fuzing radars, if it looked as if there were transmissions from enemy radars which might interfere with those fitted in the bomb. We were not worried about the deliberate jamming from the Japanese—that would have required extremely detailed a priori knowledge of our mission. The real problem was inadvertent jamming from radars.[27]

Two B-29s accompanied *Bockscar*, one carrying cameras and one with cameras and scientific monitoring equipment. The latter was *The Great Artiste*, piloted by Captain Frederick Bock, the only plane to fly over the target area on both atomic strikes. It was considered too difficult to shift the scientific gear to another plane. On board *The Great Artiste* was *New York Times* science writer William L. (Bill) Laurence, who had been "read into" the project with General Groves's permission and would fly on the Nagasaki mission.[28]

Two weather planes preceded the strike and, again, a B-29 was sent to Iwo Jima to stand by in the event that *Bockscar* encountered mechanical problems en route to Japan. The planes encountered bad weather, but no mechanical problems; however, they used more fuel than predicted.

As Major Sweeney's bomb-carrying B-29 approached the Japanese home islands, the weather planes reported that both targets were relatively clear. But as *Bockscar* neared the primary target of Kokura the weather closed in over the target—nine-tenths cloud cover was observed. Sweeney made two runs over Kokura hoping for a break in the clouds. Those maneuvers, at full power, took about

45 minutes and consumed considerable fuel. Also, there was some anti-aircraft fire, and Japanese fighters were observed climbing toward the bomber.

Sweeney, after discussions with Commander Ashworth, turned *Bockscar* in the direction of Nagasaki. Because of strong headwinds the fuel situation in *Bockscar* was becoming critical due to the plane carrying 600 gallons of unusable fuel.[29] If the plane could not immediately bomb Nagasaki, Sweeney would have to divert to the U.S.-held island of Okinawa. (The plane could be refueled on Okinawa, but there was no facility for unloading or transferring the bomb to another B-29.)

The weather was quickly closing in on Nagasaki. The bombing run was made by radar. Radio silence was broken twice during the bomb run—to see if the other B-29s could be contacted and to alert U.S. air-sea rescue forces to the possibility that *Bockscar* might have to come down at sea near a U.S. rescue ship after the bombing.

As *Bockscar* approached the release point there was a break in the clouds and the bombardier, Captain Kermit Beahan, was able to release the bomb visually at 11:58 A.M. *Bockscar* was at 31,000 feet with a ground speed of 323 mph when the Fat Man fell away. The Fat Man bomb detonated 1,650 feet above the port city with a yield of 21 kilotons. Hemmed in by hills around the impact point, the explosion caused less damage than the Hiroshima bomb.[30] Still, in the instant of explosion, thousands died; by the end of the year an estimated 70,000 who had been at Nagasaki were dead, and the city was smashed.

As the B-29s turned away, they were buffeted by five shock waves. Low on fuel, *Bockscar* and *The Great*

The mushroom-shaped cloud over Nagasaki on the morning of August 9, 1945. A third atomic bomb was in preparation for delivery on a Japanese target by the end of the month, and additional atomic bombs were being produced when the Pacific war ended shortly after the Nagasaki attack. (AAF/NASM)

The *Bockscar*, which dropped the Fat Man bomb on Nagasaki. The Nagasaki mission encountered numerous problems and at one point was almost aborted because of the aircraft's fuel situation and poor weather. This photo was taken at Roswell Army Air Field in New Mexico. (AAF/NASM)

the next Fat Man bomb to Tinian. Still, on August 14, seven of the 509th's B-29s returned to strike the Japanese cities of Koroma and Nagoya with Pumpkin bombs. A total of 741 B-29s were launched to bomb targets in Japan on August 14. Those were the last bombs dropped by B-29s in World War II.

That same day the Japanese government accepted the terms of the Potsdam Proclamation. The war was over.

Artiste headed to Okinawa to refuel before returning to Tinian. *Bockscar* touched down on Okinawa's Yontan airfield at 1:51 P.M. The aircraft had just enough fuel to taxi off the runway before the engines began sputtering. *The Great Artiste* landed immediately afterwards, followed a short time later by the *Full House*.

On Tinian the 509th ground and ordnance crews continued preparations for additional nuclear strikes. Atomic bombs of the Fat Man (plutonium) type were in production at Los Alamos; the first had been tested at Alamogordo in July, the second had been available on Tinian on August 1 and was dropped on Nagasaki. A third Fat Man (presumably F-32) could have been available on Tinian by late August. Tibbets already had decided that he would fly the third nuclear strike. It was possible Los Alamos could produce three additional Fat Man bombs in September, and the production rate was expected to increase to seven or more per month by December 1945.

But General Groves halted shipment of the final components for

FAT MAN ATOMIC BOMB

The Fat Man atomic bomb was 10⅔ feet long, and five feet in diameter and weighed 10,000 pounds. It was more complex—and more powerful—than the Little Boy bomb. The Fat Man was built around two hemispheres containing plutonium. Conventional explosives, arranged as "lenses" to produce a tightly focused implosion, drove the two hemispheres together, doubling the plutonium's density and producing the supercritical mass. The resultant chain reaction would produce an atomic explosion.

In a test—code-named Trinity—in the New Mexico wilderness on July 16, 1945, a teardrop-shaped Fat Man bomb was cradled in cables atop a 103-foot steel tower. Shortly before dawn, electrical charges detonated the explosives, and the bomb produced a blinding 18.6-kiloton explosion.

The Fat Man bomb dropped on Nagasaki had a yield of approximately 21 kilotons.

The Fat Man atomic bomb. (AAF)

B-29 POSTSCRIPTS

4

The Japanese message accepting the terms of the Potsdam Declaration was announced publicly by President Truman on the evening of August 14 in Washington. It was about 10 A.M. on August 15 in the Marianas. That evening the B-29s crews and their ground personnel in the Marianas celebrated the end of the war.

A few days later Colonel Paul Tibbets and some of his crew and the scientific staff flew to Tokyo in two of their C-54s. After contacting a Japanese physicist to discuss the effects of the atomic bombings, they traveled to Nagasaki. Tibbets and the others "walked around the city during the three days we spent there and were amazed at the extent of the destruction. Block after block had been flattened, as if by a tornado."[1]

Returning to Tinian, Tibbets and the members of the 509th Composite Group and the Manhattan Project staff packed their gear. By the end of August the first personnel were returning to the United States by ship and plane. The *Enola Gay* was one of the last B-29s to depart, making its final takeoff from Tinian's North Field on November 4. The B-29s flew to Roswell Army Air Field in New Mex-ico, the group's new home base. The *Enola Gay* touched down at Roswell on November 8. Training flights followed.

There soon would be another atomic bombing mission.

As early as 1944 the senior officials of the Manhattan Project had given serious consideration to the possibility of "testing" an atomic bomb on the Japanese Fleet at the island of Truk in a combat strike. In July 1945, General of the Army H. H. Arnold, the head of the Army Air Forces (AAF), proposed that the effects of an atomic bomb explosion on a harbor be investigated; a month later the Navy's senior expert on nuclear energy programs, Rear Admiral Lewis Strauss, suggested that nuclear weapons be tested against surplus warships.

The Navy wanted to know how atomic detonations would affect ships. What were the effects of an air blast as compared with an underwater blast? How would radiation endanger personnel aboard ship? Could existing ships be modified to survive a nuclear attack? Could a single nuclear weapon destroy a task group? A task force? To answer these and hundreds of other questions, the atomic bombing of ships was authorized late in 1945, with the tests to take place the following May at the remote Bikini atoll in

The flight crew of the B-29 *Dave's Dream* at Kwajalein in July 1946. This B-29 dropped the fourth atomic bomb, to be detonated on target ships at Bikini lagoon on July 1, 1946. Both of the Bikini atomic bombs were of the Fat Man type, as was the weapon detonated at a New Mexico test site in July 1945. (AAF)

the Marshall Islands. A joint Army-Navy-AAF task force would conduct the tests.

The U.S. Joint Chiefs of Staff directed that

> The general requirements of the test will be to determine the effects of atomic explosives against ships selected to give good representation of construction of modern naval and merchant vessels suitably disposed to give a good gradation of damage from maximum to minimum. . . . Tests should be so arranged as to take advantage of opportunities to obtain the effects of atomic explosives against ground

and air targets and to acquire scientific data of general value if this is practicable.[2]

The Bikini tests would be known as Operation Crossroads. Initially three nuclear detonations were scheduled: "Able" was to be a bomber-dropped air burst over the ship-filled lagoon, "Baker" a shallow underwater explosion, and "Charlie" a deep-water shot. Scores of outdated and damaged U.S. warships and several surrendered Axis ships would be used as target ships at Bikini. On their decks would be aircraft, vehicles, and test animals, with monitoring devices set up on the ships and nearby beaches.

The AAF would provide the B-29 for the aerial drop and extensive support for the tests. The 509th Composite Group still had the world's only nuclear-capable aircraft.[3] Colonel Tibbets was relieved of command of the group, having been in command for 18 months; however, he remained as a technical advisor to the group while continuing to command the *Enola Gay*. A bombing competition was held by the new 509th commander using dummy bomb shapes. Despite the *Enola Gay* scoring the best in the competition, the B-29 *Dave's Dream* piloted by Major Woodrow P. Swancutt was selected to drop the Fat Man bomb at Bikini. Tibbets and his crew flew the *Enola Gay* to Kwajalein Island in late April to help provide support for Operation Crossroads.

The aiming point in the center of the ship-covered lagoon was the anchored battleship *Nevada*, painted international orange and further marked with a flashing light. At 9 A.M. on July 1, *Dave's Dream*, flying 30,000 feet above the Bikini lagoon, released a 20-kiloton Fat Man atomic bomb.

The Navy had wanted to detonate this air-burst bomb from a tethered balloon to ensure accuracy. The AAF insisted on a B-29 airdrop to provide practice for the bomber crew and to demonstrate the accuracy of the bombing system. The bomb missed the aim point by 1,800 feet; the detonation damaged much of the sensitive monitoring equipment, thereby reducing the scientific usefulness of the detonation itself. The *Nevada* survived the blast, although five ships were sunk and others were severely damaged.

That same day Major General Curtis LeMay, now head of AAF research and development, met with Colonel Tibbets to determine what had gone wrong. After Tibbets explained that the bombardier of *Dave's Dream* had made incorrect calculations—which Tibbets had tried to correct before the mission—LeMay directed him to immediately fly to Washington and explain the situation to General Carl A. Spaatz, the new commanding general of the AAF. Tibbets took off an hour later in the *Enola Gay*. After landing in California, Tibbets switched to another aircraft to reach Washington.

The *Enola Gay* flew on to Roswell.

Hundreds of foreign and press representatives observed the two atomic bombs detonated at Bikini in July 1946. The targets were German, Japanese, and U.S. naval ships, many loaded with vehicles, measuring devices, and test animals. Here, the underwater bomb of Baker test erupts on July 25, 1946. Note the target ships at the edge of the explosion. (AAF)

For the Baker test at Bikini, another Fat Man atomic bomb was suspended 90 feet beneath a landing ship moored in the lagoon and detonated on July 25. A massive amount of data was obtained in tests Able and Baker, so much that test Charlie—the deep-water, 3,000-foot detonation—was postponed and then cancelled. The director of the Los Alamos laboratory, Norris Bradbury, believed that the data from the Baker test made it possible to determine the effects of a deep-water atomic explosion. Also, there were very few atomic bombs in the nation's stockpile—components existed for just seven at the time—hence, further expenditure in tests was not justified.

Meanwhile, in March–April 1946 the air staff in the Pentagon

B-29s were employed extensively as strategic reconnaissance aircraft. The F-13A (later RB-29) *Suella J.* was used at the Bikini atomic bomb tests. Here, on Kwajalein, technicians have laid out the different types of cameras that she could carry—but not all at once. The "F" in black on the tail fin indicates the 3rd Photo Reconnaissance Squadron. (AAF)

developed plans for an atomic strike force. According to the plan, the 58th Bombardment Wing was to be the nation's nuclear striking force and was "to be capable of immediate and sustained VLR [Very-Long Range] offensive operations in any part of the world, either independently or in cooperation with land and naval forces, utilizing the latest and most advanced weapons."[4] The 58th Wing was to have four very-heavy bomb groups, including the 509th Bombardment Group. Although the plan provided for 108 nuclear-capable B-29s, in fact there were only 20-odd Silverplate bombers in existence at the time.

The *Enola Gay* was not counted among the nuclear-capable B-29s for very long. In late July 1946 the *Enola Gay* was flown to Davis-Monthan Army Air Field in Arizona in preparation for placing the aircraft in storage. The aircraft was dropped from the AAF active inventory on August 30. But the *Enola Gay* was marked for historic preservation by the Air Force and, after the aircraft was reconditioned for flight, on July 3, 1949, Tibbets again took his place in the left-hand seat of the bomber and took off. The plane was flown to Park Ridge, Illinois (now O'Hare airport). In ceremonies at the airfield the *Enola Gay* was transferred to the Smithsonian Institution for eventual restoration and display. There was, however, no suitable place to display the aircraft, and it sat at Park Ridge until January 1952.

At that time, with the Korean War raging, the Air Force needed all available space at the airfield, and the *Enola Gay* was flown to Pyote AFB in Texas for temporary storage.[5] Almost a year later, in December 1953, the *Enola Gay* was flown to Andrews AFB, Maryland, near Washington, D.C., for temporary storage. Andrews was a major operating base, with the presidential aircraft among its tenants.

Although Andrews is considered a secure base, the area where the *Enola Gay* was parked had virtually no security. For several years the plane was in the open, exposed to the elements. The curious and those seeking mementos invaded the plane, tearing out instruments and other souvenirs, with birds and rodents following them into the aircraft. The *Enola Gay* stood there, abandoned and deteriorating.

In the post–World War II era B-29s performed search-and-rescue missions and supported various research programs. The former SB-29 aircraft—referred to as the Super Dumbo—carried powered lifeboats and other rescue gear that could be dropped to assist the crews of downed military and civilian aircraft. The lifeboats were 30-foot, powered craft provisioned with food, water, and a radio and lowered to the water by twin parachutes.

Several B-29s were used as electronic test platforms and to evaluate advanced bombs and guided missiles, with radio-controlled bombs being used on a limited (and ineffective) basis in the Korean War. Other B-29s carried aloft research aircraft that could not take off from the ground because of limited fuel. Launching them at high altitude from a B-29 gave the research aircraft more time in the "research envelope."

The rocket-propelled X-1, the first aircraft to break the sound barrier, was carried aloft and launched from a specially modified B-29s. The U.S. Navy also employed the B-29 to carry high-performance research aircraft. With the designation P2B-1, a Superfortress was used to carry the D-558-II Skyrocket research

A modified B-29B carrying the Bell X-1 research aircraft named *Glamorous Glennis*. This photo was taken on October 14, 1947, shortly before takeoff. When at desired altitude, the X-1 was launched and, piloted by Charles E. (Chuck) Yeager, broke the sound barrier. (USAF/NASM)

aircraft.[6] Several other B-29/P2B aircraft were acquired by the Navy for anti-submarine research.

In another civilian research project, a B-29 was modified to serve as a prototype airborne television relay in an effort to determine the feasibility of broadcasting television to remote areas from an aircraft flying at altitudes between 2,000 and 30,000 feet.[7] A B-29 was extensively modified for the "Stratovision" tests, the most prominent features of the test aircraft being a fixed antenna mast on the tail fin and a large antenna mast under the forward fuselage, which rotated 90 degrees to a position under the fuselage

The modified B-29B in flight with the X-1 nestled underneath prior to launch. B-29s were modified for various research and development projects; some of them were flown by the U.S. Navy (designated P2B) to launch research aircraft and to test equipment. (USAF/NASM)

In an unusual research project, this modified B-29B was used from 1947 to 1949 for tests of the Stratovision airborne television transmission project, developed jointly by Westinghouse Electric Corporation and Glenn L. Martin Company. The large antenna beneath the aircraft folded back for landing and take-off. (Westinghouse/Martin/ NASM)

for landing and takeoff. The B-29 flight testing occurred from December 1947 to February 1949.[8] It was determined that a single aircraft properly modified could deliver four television programs and five FM radio programs to more than 16 million listeners over a single metropolitan area. However, the scheme was not pursued because of advances in television broadcasting technology.

COLD WAR CRISIS AND CONFLICT

Superforts were still the backbone of the nation's strategic striking force into the early 1950s, although few were Silverplate aircraft. The first major crisis of the Cold War began on June 24, 1948, when Soviet forces halted all Allied road, rail, and waterborne traffic in and out of the Western sectors of Berlin, creating the Berlin Blockade. The Western Allies—Britain, France, and the United States—immediately initiated an airlift to bring food and coal into the besieged city.

On July 15, in response to the blockade, President Truman approved the deployment of 60 B-29 Superfortress bombers to bases in England.[9] Those were not nuclear-capable aircraft, although some of the B-29s that could carry nuclear weapons were deployed to Britain in mid-1949. All B-29 nuclear capability still resided with the 509th, now designated as a Medium Bomb Group. The 509th and the rest of the nation's strategic bombers were placed on 24-hour alert for overseas deployment.

The new strategic bombers included the six-engine, B-36 Peacemaker, which was designated a heavy bomber. In 1948 the Air Force took delivery of the first B-36, as well as the first B-50A medium bomber. The latter was an upgraded B-29, originally the B-29D, which was redesignated B-50 in 1946. Neither the initial B-36s nor the B-50s were nuclear capable at that time.

The first of the 60 B-29s arrived in England on July 17. While U.S. public statements were ambiguous about their having nuclear capability, Soviet spies in the British government had already advised Moscow that they were not "atomic bombers." The blockade ended in May 1949, although the airlift continued until September 1949. The B-29s deployed to England flew training missions and, in reality, had no effect on the international crisis.

Meanwhile, B-29s were being employed in a number of research and reconnaissance roles and to demonstrate the potential striking range of the Air Force. On July 22, 1948, three B-29s departed Davis-Monthan AFB in Arizona on the first postwar, around-the-world flight. One B-29 crashed into the Arabian Sea, with the two others returning to Davis-Monthan on August 6 after the 20,000-mile flight. The aircraft made eight en route stops; the actual flight time was 103 hours, 50 minutes.

A more sensational flight followed when, on February 26, 1949, the B-50A Superfortress *Lucky Lady II* took off from Carswell AFB (Fort Worth), Texas, on history's first nonstop around-the-world flight. The plane was refueled four times in flight by KB-29 tanker aircraft—over the Azores, Saudi Arabia, the Philippines, and Hawaii. Captain James Gallagher, the aircraft commander, brought the plane down on March 2. The plane had flown 23,452 miles in 94 hours, 1 minute, winning the coveted Mackay Trophy for the 14-man crew.

The tanker-configured KB-29s were invaluable for extending the range of combat aircraft, both bombers and fighters. Older B-29s were fitted initially with flexible hoses and, subsequently, with rigid-boom refueling capabilities. And Superforts were increasingly being used for reconnaissance. In the late 1940s only RB-29s were available for long-range (strategic) photo missions. As the secrecy of the Soviet Union forced U.S. military and political leaders to approve missions along the coasts of Soviet bloc countries and later the coast of China, the RB-29s were particularly useful because of their great endurance. For example, in 1948 camera-fitted RB-29s taking off from Alaska crossed the Bering Strait to take oblique photos of the Chukotski Peninsula in the Soviet Far East. These RB-29s could fly for up to 30 hours without aerial refueling.

Another type of reconnaissance role was filled by the WB-29, configured for long-range weather reporting. On September 3, 1949, a WB-29 weather aircraft flying from Japan to Alaska on an atmospheric sampling mission detected the first signs of Soviet nuclear tests. Analysis of the air samples determined that "there was no room for doubt that an atomic explosion had occurred somewhere on the Asiatic mainland and at some date between 26 and 29 August."[10] The Soviet Union had detonated its first nuclear weapon on August 25, 1949.

The B-29s returned to combat in the summer of 1950 after Soviet-supported North Korean troops crossed the 38th Parallel to invade South Korea on June 25. At the time there was a B-29 bomb group on Guam; two more groups were rapidly deployed to Kadena Air Base on Okinawa and Yokota Air Base in Japan.

The B-29 Superfortress was among the first U.S. aircraft fitted for in-flight refueling as the Air Force sought to extend the range of strategic bombers to reach the Soviet heartland. The B-29 tanker (above) refuels a bomber with a flexible hose in an early test. The lower aircraft carries the arrowhead-in-a-circle insignia of the 509th. (U.S. Air Force)

The Air Force soon shifted to the rigid flying boom for refueling, as shown here on a KB-29 tanker. The assembly at the tail holds the boom when not in use. All guns have been removed from the tanker and the bomb bays replaced by fuel tanks. The radar dome under the fuselage is visible. (USAF)

Late in the afternoon of June 28, four B-29s from Okinawa began bombing targets of opportunity along Korean highways and railroad tracks. To quote the U.S. Air Force official history, "it was a strange employment for the strategic bombers, but General [Douglas] MacArthur had called for a maximum show of force."[11] It was a beginning, and in the coming three years of war, only 26 days would not record B-29 missions over Korea.

The first large-scale B-29 strike came on July 13, 1950, when 50 B-29s struck Wonsan, North Korea. Initially, there was no air opposition, and Air Force planners were emboldened to

A B-29 bomber about to "plug in" to a KB-29 tanker. The refueling receptacle is located between the cockpit and the forward dorsal turret (mounting four .50-caliber machine guns). In-flight refueling, which requires great pilot skill, is now an everyday occurrence for military aircraft. (USAF)

the State Department quickly declared Wojin temporarily off limits to "strategic" bombers.

Other missions were more successful. On August 25, 1951—with Navy carrier-based fighters for escort—29 B-29s returned to previously off-limits Wojin. Bombing visually, the B-29s dropped 97 percent of their bombs on target, wiping out the city's railroad marshaling yards. (One bomber jettisoned a string of bombs at sea, just missing a U.S. cruiser and two destroyers that were standing offshore.)

The entry of Chinese ground and air forces into the Korean War in the winter of 1950–1951 led to jet-propelled fighter opposition to the B-29s strikes. The Soviet-built MiG-15 fighters threatened the bombers, requiring U.S. Air Force and Navy to provide fighter escorts.[12] But the B-29 missions continued despite increasing losses.

The Korean War also saw a major increase in U.S. military interest in photo-reconnaissance. The Air Force flew mostly RB-29s and turbojet RB-45C Tornado aircraft for long-range reconnaissance of North Korea. Those planes also required fighter escorts to protect them from the Chinese MiG-15 interceptors that inundated the North Korean skies from the fall of 1950. There were several attacks on U.S. reconnaissance aircraft, with some being damaged and two RB-29s probably shot down during the conflict.

On June 13, 1952, an RB-29 disappeared while on a reconnaissance mission over the Sea of Japan, leaving no trace of the aircraft or its 12 crewmen. A Soviet fighter attack was reported by some sources. On October 7, 1952, Soviet fighters shot down another RB-29 on a routine flight off the coast of Japan; eight crewmen were lost.

The U.S. Air Force and Navy lost several reconnaissance aircraft during the 1950s, after the war ended. One was an RB-29, shot down by Soviet fighters near Hokkaido, Japan, on November 7, 1954. Ten crewmen were rescued, and one was lost.

With the end of the Korean War, Chinese arms and technical advisors were transferred to Indochina to help the Communist Viet Minh in their conflict against the French. When French forces were surrounded by Communist troops in the valley of Dien Bien Phu in April 1954, U.S. officials began planning Operation Vautour ("Vulture")—the intervention of U.S. air forces in the Indochina War. There were many variations of the plan, with one providing for all 98 B-29 Superfortress bombers in the Far East to use conventional bombs to destroy the Viet Minh forces around the besieged French troops. Reportedly, some variations of the plan called for the use of a nuclear weapon to be dropped by either a B-50 or, more likely, by a Navy carrier-based aircraft. Using the latter would avoid the political problems of having a nuclear-armed aircraft take off from a land base in the Pacific area.

President Dwight D. Eisenhower decided against U.S. intervention in Indochina. The besieged French troops at Dien Bien Phu were decimated by Viet Minh artillery barrages and human-wave assaults. With most French positions overrun by the Communist troops, the survivors surrendered on May 7, 1954. The defeat led France to abandon Indochina, with the United States accepting sponsorship of the portion that became South Vietnam.

By the early 1950s the B-29 bombers and photo planes were being phased out of U.S. service. The more capable B-50 Superfortress would serve a few more years, while the KB-29 tankers would outlast them all, the last being grounded in 1956.

One other B-29 carrier configuration warrants attention: the "parasite" fighter concept. During the 1950s the Air Force developed the FICON (Fighter Conveyor) program in which an RB-36 could carry, launch, and recover an RF-84 Thunderstreak reconnaissance aircraft. An earlier version of this concept was a plan to carry a diminutive fighter to protect the RB-36 from enemy interceptors. During flight tests the fighter, the turbojet XF-85 Goblin, which had a gross weight of only 4,850 pounds, was carried aloft, released, and recovered from a B-29 fitted with a special trapeze-like device. (The bomb bays were modified and the doors removed

COLD WAR B-29/B-50 SUPERFORTRESS STRENGTH

	B-29	RB-29*	KB-29	B-50	RB-50
1946	148	few	—	—	—
1947	319	few	—	—	—
1948	486	30	—	35	—
1949	390	62	67	99	—
1950	286	46	126	196	19
1951	340	30	187	219	40
1952	417	18	179	224	39
1953	110	8	143	138	38
1954	—	—	91	78	12
1955	—	—	82	—	12
1956	—	—	74	—	—

*Designated F-13 until 1948.

for the tests.) While the RB-36/RF-84 program produced an operational capability, only two XF-85s were built, and the program never reached fruition.

The B-29 bombers and reconnaissance aircraft were replaced in the U.S. Air Force by the giant B-36s and the far more effective jet-propelled B-47 Stratojet and B-52 Stratofortress bombers. Strategic reconnaissance was being carried out by variants of the jet bombers, as well as the very versatile RB-57 Canberra and the highly secret U-2 spyplane. The KC-97 piston-engine tankers carried on after the KB-29s left service, but coming into service was the jet-propelled KC-135, vital to the effective refueling of modern bombers.

Three other countries also flew B-29-type bombers: Great Britain, the Soviet Union, and China. The B-29 was the first U.S. aircraft to enter squadron service with the Royal Air Force (RAF) after World War II. By the late 1940s the RAF long-range striking force was limited to a few squadrons of piston-engine Lincolns, successor to the most effective Lancaster. Due to financial constraints, no suitable British bomber was available to the RAF for several years, pending delivery of the jet-propelled V-bombers.[13] Accordingly, 88 B-29 Superfortresses were taken out of U.S. Air Force storage, modernized, and transferred to the RAF. As the Washington B.1, they were in RAF service from 1950 to early 1958; they were not configured for carrying nuclear weapons.[14]

THE SOVIET SUPERFORTRESS

A plane closely resembling the B-29 was flown in large numbers by Soviet Long-Range Aviation (LRA). This was the Tu-4, which was copied from three AAF B-29s that had landed in Soviet Siberia in late 1944 after bombing raids against Manchuria and Japan (at the time the Soviet Union was neutral in the Pacific war). The aircraft were interned and Andrei N. Tupolev, the doyen of Soviet bomber designers, was assigned the highest priority to produce an exact copy of the Boeing B-29 suitable for mass production. One of the B-29s was broken down, and its components and materials studied; the two other B-29s were employed for trials and training. In fact, an exact copy was not possible because of the Soviet use of metric measures and the lack of certain components, especially the engines and tires, as well as the need to modify the bomb bays to accommodate Soviet weapons.[15]

The story is told that Tupolev, instructed by Soviet security intelligence chief Lavrenty Beria to produce an exact copy of the B-29s, was forced to ask if the planes were to have the American or Soviet insignia painted on them! Tupolev succeeded in his task, and in record time. The first Soviet B-29 copy flew on May 19, 1947 (the Tu-70 transport version having flown six months earlier). Three Tu-4s participated in the Soviet Aviation Day display over Moscow's Tushino airport on August 3, 1947, accompanied by the Tu-70 transport. Series production was already underway. The Soviets built 20 preproduction aircraft at GAZ No. 124 at

One of the first views that Western intelligence had of the Tu-4 "Bull" copy of the B-29 was in a Soviet newsreel. The aircraft was an almost exact copy of the B-29 Superfortress and would provide the USSR with its first aircraft capable of carrying an atomic bomb. (USAF)

Kazan.[16] Full-scale production followed with some 300 aircraft completed by 1950 and total production numbering about 400 aircraft.

Given the U.S. military reporting name Bull, this was the first Soviet bomber capable of carrying an atomic bomb and the first bomber with sufficient range to reach the United States, albeit on a one-way bombing mission. The so-called eighth series aircraft (1949) were the first fitted to carry an atomic bomb and with the Kobalt

bombing radar in a retractable dome mounted between the bomb bays. (Earlier Tu-4s did not have radar.) Although the aircraft were fitted to carry an atomic bomb from 1949, practical weapons were not available for the aircraft until 1953.

Aviation historian Bill Gunston, in his comprehensive study of Tupolev aircraft, wrote:

> The story of the Tu-4 is without parallel in technological history. It is the story of how what has been correctly described as "the most complicated moving machine created by man up to that time" was appropriated without permission of the owners, dismantled and dissected in the most minute detail, to the extent of analysing all the materials used, and then copied in a form which was put into series production in the Soviet Union. It was the first and greatest example of what today is called "reverse engineering."[17]

Variants of the Tu-4 were configured for long-range photo-reconnaissance (Tu-4R) and as aerial tankers as well as for various research-and-development configurations. The Tu-4 was used for in-flight refueling experiments to extend the bomber's range, serving as both tanker and receiver aircraft; at least 12 aircraft were converted between 1952 and 1955 to tanker configurations. The Tu-4T was a one-of-a-kind assault transport for carrying 28 paratroopers, and another was converted to carry 52 troops. The Tu-4 served in Soviet LRA well into the late 1950s with some aircraft also flown by Soviet Naval Aviation.

During the 1950s several Tu-4s were transferred to the Chinese Air Force, undoubtedly providing China's first nuclear delivery platform.

A row of Tu-4 strategic bombers on a snow-covered Soviet airfield. The brilliant aircraft designer Andrei N. Tupolev made an almost exact replica of the B-29, using as models three U.S. bombers that landed in Siberia during World War II. There were differences in the engines, landing gear, and defensive weapons because of Soviet production limitations.

The USSR presented China with several Tu-4 aircraft. This one was employed as a test bed for an AEW configuration. There are electronic pods beneath the fuselage, and the horizontal tail has been modified; there is a large "saucer" structure atop the plane that would house a rotating radar antenna. (Richard Hallion)

Some reports contend that Stalin presented Mao Tse-tung with ten of the bombers for his 60th birthday, which were delivered in February 1953. Three more aircraft were transferred to China the following year. A Tu-4 was seen to take off from Zhengzhou (formerly Chengchow) in 1985. The Chinese also fitted at least one Tu-4 as a test bed for Airborne Early Warning (AEW) development, although an operating radar was not installed.[18]

Thus, the last aircraft of the B-29 design in military service was flown by the Chinese Air Force. Civilian-owned B-29s continue to fly in the United States.

THE ARTIFACT

The *Enola Gay* is the largest military aircraft artifact preserved by the National Air and Space Museum. It has also been one of the largest and most complex restoration projects in the history of aviation.

When the Smithsonian Institution accepted custody of the *Enola Gay* in 1949, it intended to display the aircraft someday, but the nation's aviation museum at that time was a Nissen hut on the Mall in Washington, D.C. Indeed, 45 years would elapse between the Smithsonian Institution's taking title to the aircraft—albeit not possession—and its being placed on display. From 1949 to 1960 the *Enola Gay* was stored at various Air Force bases. Finally, in August 1960, technicians from the Smithsonian's restoration facility at Silver Hill (Suitland), Maryland, began disassembling the aircraft as it stood in the open at Andrews AFB. The fuselage had to be separated into two parts, the engines removed, and the wings broken down into sections. It took almost a year to take the plane apart and to move the sections by truck to the Silver Hill facility, which was named for Paul E. Garber in 1980. There the *Enola Gay*'s sections could be safeguarded until funding and manpower were available to restore the aircraft.

Limited resources became available to begin restoration in late 1984, with the plan being to display portions of the aircraft at the new National Air and Space Museum on the Mall or possibly at Dulles International Airport some 25 miles west of Washington. It was estimated that restoration could take a full decade. It was hoped that the work could be accomplished by the 50th anniversary of the *Enola Gay*'s historic mission.

From the outset Smithsonian officials realized that it would be extremely difficult to place the fully assembled aircraft on display. As originally proposed in the 1960s, a new museum was to have been large enough to accommodate both the *Enola Gay* and the U.S. Navy flying boat *NC-4*, the two largest aircraft in the museum's collection in terms of wingspan.[1] However, the new museum's proposed size was reduced due to a shortfall in the funds Congress approved for its construction. The fully assembled *Enola Gay* would not fit into the museum without the displacement of many other aircraft; nor could the museum's floors accept the weight of the assembled bomber.

Still, some portion of the bomber would be placed on public display, hopefully in the summer of 1995 to coincide with the 50th anniversary of the end of World War II. Extensive planning was required on the part of the Garber staff and museum curators. Work on the plane began in January 1985. Teams from the Garber staff were assigned to each section of the aircraft. Numerous volunteers and interns would also participate in the restoration. One volunteer had flown as a flight engineer on B-29s and brought first-hand knowledge to the project. Lin Ezell, in charge of the Garber facility during much of the restoration process, noted that everyone at the facility worked on the *Enola Gay*—"the magnitude of the project has led everyone to be a participant . . . we're shy on resources and something this large has had to have everyone's support. It means other special projects and favorite projects have had to go to the back burner."[2]

The Garber staff pored over documents and photographs of the *Enola Gay*. Fortunately, members of the *Enola Gay*'s crew, as well as men who had flown other B-29s, came to Garber to look at the aircraft and answer questions about the plane's condition and appearance in 1945. Thousands of photographs of B-29s, technical and maintenance manuals, and logbooks were available to guide the staff. And experience in rebuilding other aircraft gave the Garber specialists a feel for the aircraft so that they could identify post–August 1945 modifications and equipment changes.

Each section and portion of the aircraft had to be taken apart. All wiring and tubing and each part and component were removed. An inventory was made, and parts were photographed and labeled so that the plane—which soon resembled a huge jigsaw puzzle—could be reassembled. The pieces of the puzzle were countless. One intern recalled the

extreme amount of care that goes into the very tiny things—I have spent . . . hours just doing hardware, nuts and bolts, restoring nuts and bolts and washers, that are original to the B-29 *Enola Gay*, [restoring them] to a condition that they can be put back on and used.[3]

The parts and components had to be cleaned. Heat, cold, and bird droppings, as well as operational wear and tear, had affected virtually all parts of the aircraft. Some parts and instruments had been removed from the aircraft before it reached Garber. When parts could not be restored or were missing, the Garber staff sought out replacements from other sources or, as a last resort, fabricated exact replacements in the facility's workshops. Fabricated parts were so marked to enable future aviation curators and historians to differentiate them from the original *Enola Gay* components.

Two of the Wright R-3350 engines were completely rebuilt at the Garber facility; the two others were rehabilitated at the San Diego Aerospace Museum. Special fluids were used where appropriate in oil, gasoline, and hydraulic lines to help preserve them.

PAUL E. GARBER PRESERVATION, RESTORATION, AND STORAGE FACILITY

The Garber facility is located in Silver Hill (Suitland), Maryland, a suburb of Washington, D.C. That is where the B-29 *Enola Gay* was restored for display at the National Air and Space Museum's Dulles facility. The 30-odd buildings of the Garber facility were used for artifact storage and document and photo collections and as workshops for the restoration of aviation and space artifacts.

A staff of some 50 specialists, supported by administrative and security personnel, maintained and restored a great number of the artifacts of the National Air and Space Museum. A large force of volunteers and interns assisted the professional staff.

The Garber facility was named for the late Paul E. Garber, who was a driving force in expanding the Smithsonian Institution's aeronautical collection during his 72-year association with the institution.

Meanwhile, plans were initiated in the 1980s to display the *Enola Gay* at the National Air and Space Museum. Subsequently, discussions were initiated at the museum that led to the decision to display the *Enola Gay* in the context of the history of strategic bombing in an exhibit tentatively entitled "From Guernica to Hiroshima: Strategic Bombing in World War II."[4] A colloquium series on strategic bombing was proposed in conjunction with the exhibit. Surviving participants of the U.S. Strategic Bombing Survey, which had examined the effects of strategic bombing in World War II, and senior officials of the Cold War era would be invited to participate.

The exhibit itself would have several hundred captioned photos to illustrate strategic bombing and, especially, the atomic bombing of Japan. Then, the visitors would be exposed to portions of the *Enola Gay* and other artifacts from the 509th Composite Group. However, circulation of the draft scripts for the exhibit unleashed a firestorm of protest. Numerous critics cited a lack of balance, believing the exhibit to disparage U.S. strategic bombing of Japan without putting the B-29 campaign into proper perspective or properly addressing the question of why the atomic bombs were used. As a result of the controversy, Smithsonian officials decided to reduce the exhibit to the *Enola Gay* alone—the aircraft, the crew, and the Hiroshima mission of August 6, 1945.

Finally, the staff, volunteers, and interns at the Garber facility completed their Herculean task on those portions of the bomber that would be displayed. Every nut, screw, washer, and bolt and every major section and part had been returned to pristine condition, or a new part had been fitted that was virtually indistinguishable from the original. The assembled sections were polished and repolished until they gleamed as they had when the bomber rolled off the production line a half-century earlier. About 44,000 working hours had been spent on the restoration.

ON DISPLAY AT LAST

At night during May and June 1995, large trucks drove through the streets of Washington to unloaded their cargo into gallery 103 of the National Air and Space Museum, between Independence Avenue and the Mall. Placed on exhibit was the forward portion of the *Enola Gay* fuselage, 56 feet in length, including the two bomb bays. Beneath the fuselage was a casing for a Little Boy atomic bomb. Two of the plane's engines, a propeller, and the vertical stabilizer (tail fin), the last emblazoned with the circle-R marking, as well as other *Enola Gay* and 509th Composite Group artifacts were placed nearby in the gallery. A part of the exhibit included a brief film on the restoration of the aircraft, and a 16½-minute video film titled "The *Enola Gay*: The First Atomic Mission," made specifically for the museum, was shown in a small theater setting.[5]

The *Enola Gay* exhibit was opened to the public on June 28, 1995. More than 3,200 visitors went through gallery 103 on that first day. Within a month, more than 97,000 visitors had walked through the gallery. Long lines of visitors continued to form before the museum opened its doors, waiting to see the *Enola Gay*. Hundreds of thousands of visitors saw the *Enola Gay* at the National Air and Space Museum.

In preparation for major repairs to the Air and Space Museum, the *Enola Gay* exhibit was closed on May 18, 1998. Work on restoration continued at the Garber facility, and the plane has been fully assembled and is now on display in the museum's Dulles facility, which opened on December 15, 2003. Thus, for the first time, this milestone of flight is on public display in its entirety.

The *Enola Gay* is important to history as the aircraft that dropped the first atomic bomb used in combat. It is also a representation of the B-29 Superfortress program, one of the most

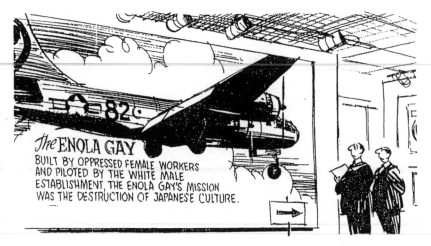

The ENOLA GAY
BUILT BY OPPRESSED FEMALE WORKERS AND PILOTED BY THE WHITE MALE ESTABLISHMENT, THE ENOLA GAY'S MISSION WAS THE DESTRUCTION OF JAPANESE CULTURE.

"I think the Smithsonian's getting carried away with this historical revisionism . . ."

The controversy over the *Enola Gay* exhibition at the National Air and Space Museum that opened in 1995 led to a barrage of political cartoons. This one by Henry Payne and that by Stuart Carlson were among the most poignant published. (United Features Syndicate)

The Stuart Carlson cartoon. (Universal Press Syndicate)

The *Enola Gay* being assembled at the Steven F. Udvar-Hazy Center at Dulles International Airport outside of Washington, D.C. In this view the fuselage is about to be moved back some 20 feet to mate with the wing section. The *Enola Gay* is the largest military aircraft at the museum. (Eric Long/NASM)

The *Enola Gay*—completely reassembled and ready for the public. (Eric Long/NASM)

advanced aircraft and impressive production efforts of its time. As part of the wall text of the 1995 *Enola Gay* exhibit stated,

the use of the bombs led to the immediate surrender of Japan and made unnecessary the planned invasion of the Japanese home islands. Such an invasion, especially if un- dertaken for the main islands, would have led to very heavy casualties among American and Allied troops and Japanese civilians and military. It was thought highly un- likely that Japan, while in a very weakened military condi- tion, would have surrendered unconditionally without such an invasion.

THE NATIONAL AIR AND SPACE MUSEUM

The National Air and Space Museum, located on the Mall in Wash- ington, D.C., is visited by almost ten million people every year, significantly more than visit any other museum in the world.

The museum traces its beginning to a congressional act of Au- gust 12, 1946, which established a national air museum to memo- rialize the national development of aviation; collect, preserve, and display aeronautical equipment of historical interest and signifi- cance; serve as a repository for scientific equipment and data per- taining to the development of aviation; and provide educational material for the historical study of aviation.

At the time there was no national air museum. Rather, aircraft models and aviation memorabilia were displayed in a Nissen hut on the Mall. Actual artifacts were displayed in the Arts and Indus- tries Building. Charles Lindbergh's *Spirit of Saint Louis* was placed on display in 1928, and the *Wright Flyer*, which the Wright broth- ers flew at Kitty Hawk, North Carolina, in 1903, was acquired by the Smithsonian in 1948 and placed on display.

In 1958 Congress authorized the construction of an air museum building, although it did not vote to spend the $40 million to construct a museum building on the Mall until 1972. Meanwhile, in 1966, President Lyndon B. Johnson signed Public Law 89–509, which amended the original air museum legisla- tion to include the field of space flight and changed the mu- seum's name to the National Air and Space Museum.

The new building, a large, three-story structure located be- tween Jefferson Drive and Independence Avenue, was opened by President Gerald Ford on July 1, 1976, a few days before the 200th anniversary of the Declaration of Independence.

The museum is open to the public, free of charge, every day of the year except December 25. Beyond the galleries of aviation and space artifacts, the museum has several theaters that show air- and space-related films, a planetarium, and—for the researcher and student—a major library and photograph collection.

The massive Dulles center, named for benefactor Steven F. Udvar-Hazy, was opened on December 11, 2003, commemo- rating the 100th anniversary of the Wright brothers' flight at Kitty Hawk.

APPENDIX A
Enola Gay Chronology

Asterisks indicate bombing missions (practice and combat) in which the *Enola Gay* participated; the *Enola Gay*'s aircraft commander is indicated for those missions. All 509th Composite Group bombing missions over Japan are listed.

1944

March 11 393rd Bombardment Squadron (Very Heavy) activated.

December 17 509th Composite Group activated.

1945

May 9 Colonel Paul Tibbets selects B-29 No. 44–86292 as his personal aircraft at the Martin aircraft factory in Omaha, Nebraska.

May 18 B-29 No. 44–86292 is delivered to the AAF at the Martin factory.

June 14 No. 44–86292 is ferried to Wendover Army Air Field in Utah, piloted by Captain Robert A. Lewis.

June 27 Departs Wendover for Tinian, piloted by Captain Lewis.

July 6 Arrives at Guam; after additional modifications to the bomb bay, the aircraft flies on to Tinian.

July 12* Training flights from Tinian begin; practice bombing mission to Rota Island with 1,000-pound bombs; Captain James Price is aircraft commander.

July 19* Practice bombing mission to Guguan Island with 1,000-pound bombs; Captain Lewis is aircraft commander.

July 20 Ten 509th B-29s attack Japanese cities of Koriyama, Fukushima, Nagaoka, and Toyama with Pumpkin bombs (missions 1 through 4).

July 21* Practice bombing mission to Marcus Island with 500-pound bombs; Captain Lewis is aircraft commander.

July 22* Practice bombing mission with 1,000-pound bombs; 1st Lieutenant Charles McKnight is aircraft commander.

July 24* Ten 509th B-29s attack Japanese cities of Kobe, Sumitomo, and Yokkaichi with Pumpkin bombs (missions 5 through 7); aircraft commander is Captain Lewis.

July 26* Ten 509th B-29s attack Japanese cities of Nagaoka and Toyama with Pumpkin bombs (missions 8 and 9); Captain Lewis is aircraft commander.

July 29 Eight 509th B-29s attack Japanese cities of Koriyama, Ube, and Yokkaichi with Pumpkin bombs (missions 10 through 12).

July 31* Test drop of Little Boy atomic bomb shape; Colonel Tibbets is aircraft commander.

August 5 B-29 No. 44–86292 formally named *Enola Gay*; Little Boy atomic bomb is loaded.

August 6*	Atomic bombing mission against Hiroshima, piloted by Colonel Tibbets. The aircraft departs Tinian at 2:45 A.M.; the Little Boy bomb is released over Hiroshima at 8:15 A.M.; the aircraft returns to Tinian at 2:58 P.M., a flight of 12 hours, 13 minutes (mission 13).
August 8	Six 509th B-29s attack Japanese cities of Osaka and Yokkaichi with Pumpkin bombs (missions 14 and 15).
August 9	*Bockscar* attacks Nagasaki with Fat Man atomic bomb (mission 16).
August 14	Seven 509th B-29s attack Japanese cities of Koroma and Nagoya (missions 17 and 18).
November 4	*Enola Gay* departs Tinian for Roswell Army Air Field, New Mexico.
November 8	Arrives at Roswell.

1946

April 18	Departs Roswell for Operation Crossroads, piloted by Colonel Tibbets.
April 29	Arrives at Kwajalein Island to participate in Operation Crossroads.
July	509th Composite Group is redesignated 509th Bombardment Group (Very Heavy).
July 1	*Enola Gay* departs Kwajalein to return to the United States.
July 2	Arrives at Fairfield-Suisun Army Air Field, California (now Travis Air Force Base).
July 24	Flown to Davis-Monthan Army Air Field, Arizona, for storage.
August 30	Dropped from AAF inventory.

1949

| July 3 | Retrieved from storage and flown to Park Ridge (Chicago), Illinois, by Colonel Tibbets and formally transferred to the Smithsonian Institution. |

1952

| January 12 | Flown to Pyote AFB, Texas, for temporary storage. |

1953

| December 2 | Flown to Andrews AFB, Suitland, Maryland, for storage. |

1960

| August 10 | Work begins to disassemble aircraft and truck components to the Garber restoration facility in Suitland, Maryland. |

1984

| December 5 | Restoration project begins at Garber facility. |

1995

| June 28 | *Enola Gay* exhibit opens at the National Air and Space Museum, Washington, D.C. |

1998

| May 18 | *Enola Gay* exhibit closes. |

2003

| December 11 | Steven F. Udvar-Hazy Center at Dulles International Airport opens with the fully assembled *Enola Gay* on display. |

APPENDIX B

B-29 Models and Variants

Production numbers for the B-29 program vary, even among official sources. The following production totals are based on Marcelle Size Knaack, *Post-World War II Bombers 1945–1973*, Vol. II of *Encyclopedia of U.S. Air Force Aircraft and Missile Systems* (Washington, D.C.: Office of Air Force History, 1988), pp. 485–486, and Peter M. Bowers, *Boeing Aircraft Since 1916* (London: Putnam, 1989), pp. 318–340.

B-50 Superfortress production is included for comparative purposes, that aircraft being a variant of the B-29.

B-29 Production

XB-29	3	
B-29 prototypes	14	
B-29/B-29A	3,632	
B-29B	311	(B-29 total 3,960)

At the end of World War II, orders for more than 5,000 B-29s were cancelled.

B-29D/B-50A	79	
B-50B	45	
YB-50C	1	
B-50D	222	
TB-50H	24	(B-50 total 371)

B-29 variants

The suffix letters I and O are not used in aircraft designations.

XB-29	Prototype aircraft; first flight September 21, 1942.
B-29	Production aircraft; first flight June 26, 1943. *Note:* The 14 service test aircraft were sometimes referred to as YB-29.
B-29A	Production aircraft; modified wings and improved engines; fitted with four (vice two) machine guns in forward dorsal turret.
B-29B	Production aircraft; 2,000 pounds lighter with removal of all guns except tail turret, providing a slight increase in altitude and range.
B-29C	1 aircraft intended for upgraded engines; project cancelled.
B-29D	Redesignated B-50A in December 1945.
XB-29E	Aircraft modified for fire control tests; 1 aircraft modified in 1946.
B-29F	Aircraft modified for arctic operations; 6 aircraft modified.
XB-29G	Engine test aircraft with retractable turbojet in bomb bay; 1 aircraft modified.

XB-29H	Armament test aircraft; 1 aircraft modified.
YR/RB-29J	Improved reconnaissance aircraft; 6 aircraft modified.
YKB-29J	Prototype flying-boom tankers; 2 modified from RB-29J in 1948.
CB-29K	Aircraft stripped for cargo; 1 modified in 1949.
B-29L	Initial designation for KB-29M.
KB-29M	Tankers with hose-and-drogue configuration; 92 aircraft modified from 1948.
B-29MR	Standard bomber aircraft fitted for in-flight refueling from KB-29Ms; 74 modified.
B-29N	Designation apparently not used.
KB-29P	Tankers with flying boom configuration; 116 aircraft modified.
B-29Q/R/S	Designations apparently not used.
YKB-29T	Triple-point tanker aircraft; 1 modified from KB-29M.
QB-29	Radio-controlled drone; several modified from 1954.
RB-29	Photograph reconnaissance aircraft; approximately 120 aircraft modified. *Note:* Designated F-13 until 1948.
SB-29	Search-and-rescue variant; fitted with large, air-dropped lifeboat; 16 modified.
TB-29	Aircraft modified for training and target tow.
VB-29	Aircraft modified for executive transport role.
WB-29	Aircraft modified to carry meteorological equipment.
YB-39YB-29	Refitted with in-line piston engines.
XB-44B-29A	Refitted with improved engines; initially redesignated B-29D; changed to B-50A.
F-13	See RB-29 above.
P2B	Navy designation for B-29s acquired for research projects; 4 aircraft acquired (1 P2B-1, 1 P2B-1S, 2 P2B-2S), with the S suffix indicating anti-submarine warfare.
B.1	British designation for 88 B-29/B-29A aircraft; named Washington.

APPENDIX C

B-29 Characteristics

Standard Aircraft Characteristics

BY AUTHORITY OF
THE SECRETARY
OF THE AIR FORCE

B-29-
SUPERFORTRESS
Boeing

FOUR R-3350-57or-57A

WRIGHT

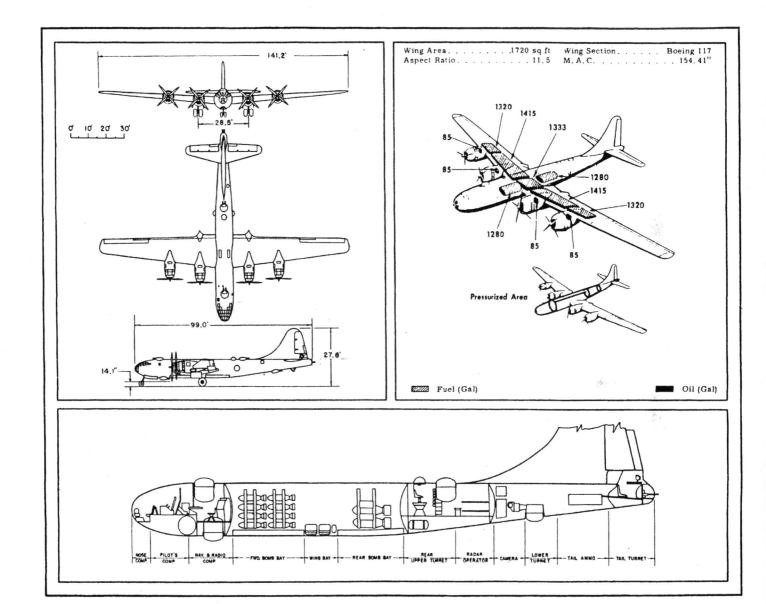

Wing Area . . . . .1720 sq ft   Wing Section . . . . . . Boeing 117
Aspect Ratio . . . . 11.5   M.A.C. . . . . 154.41"

Pressurized Area

░░░ Fuel (Gal)   ▇▇ Oil (Gal)

NOSE COMP | PILOT'S COMP | NAV. & RADIO COMP | FWD. BOMB BAY | WING BAY | REAR BOMB BAY | REAR UPPER TURRET | RADAR OPERATOR | CAMERA | LOWER TURRET | TAIL AMMO | TAIL TURRET

POWER PLANT

No. & Model .(4) R-3350-57 or 57A
Mfr .... Wright
Engine Spec No. 787-C
Superch .... 1 stg, 1 spd
Turbo Superch..... B-11 or B-31
Turbo Mfr ..... General Electric
Red. Gear Ratio 0.350
Prop Mfr .... Hamilton Std
Blade Design No. 6521A-6
Prop Type ... C.S., F.F,Hydr.
No. Blades 4
Prop Dia .... 16'7"

ENGINE RATINGS

BHP - RPM - ALT - MIN

T.O: 2200 - 2800 - S.L. - 5

Mil: 2200 - 2600 - Turbo - 30

Nor: 2000 - 2400 - Turbo - Cont.

Mission and Description

Navy Equivalent: P2B-1   Mfr's Model: 345-3-0

The principal mission of the B-29 is the destruction of enemy materiel and installations by aerial bombardment. It is provided with pressurized crew compartments and adequate heating and oxygen facilities for long range missions. Crew of 11 consists of pilot, co-pilot, flight engineer, navigator, radio operator, radar operator, bombardier and four gunners.

Direct current electrical power is supplied by six engine driven generators and one auxiliary power plant.

Early models are equipped with transfer type fuel systems while later models use the manifold type system.

Armament provided consists of five (5) turrets controlled by a central fire control system.

In later aircraft a formation stick was added to the C-1 auto-pilot to facilitate formation flying.

Development

Design initiated: . . . . Jun 40
First flight: . . . . (XB-29) Sep 42
First acceptance: . . . . Sep 43
Production completed: . . . . Jun 46

WEIGHTS

Loading	Lb	L.F.
Empty	71,500(A)	
Basic	74,050(A)	
Design	120,000	2.67
Combat	*101,082	3.10
Max T.O.		
(Overload)......	†140,000	2.28
Max T.O (Normal)	†133,500	
Max Land	‡135,000	2.35

(A) Actual
* For Basic Mission
† Limited by performance
‡ Limited by strength

FUEL

Location	No. Tanks	Gal
Wg, outbd*	2	2640
Wg, inbd*	2	2830
Wg, ctr*	1	1333
Bomb bay*	2	2560
	Total	9363
Grade		100/130
Specification		MIL-F-5572

OIL

Nacelles .... 4 ..... (tot) 340
Grade S-1120; W-1100
Specification MIL-O-6082
*Self-Sealing

DIMENSIONS

Wing
  Span .... 141.2'
  Incidence .... 4°
  Dihedral .... 4°29'
  Sweepback(LE) .... 7°1'
Length .... 99.0'
Height .... 27.8'
Tread .... 28.5'
Prop. Grd Clearance ...... 14.1"

BOMBS

No.	Lb	Type
4	4000	G.P.
8	2000	G.P.
12	1600	A.P.
12	1000	G.P.
40	500	G.P.

Max Bomb Load .... 20,000 lb

GUNS

No.	Size	Rds ea	Location
4	.50	500	Fus, upr, fwd
2	.50	500	Fus, upr, aft
2	.50	500	Fus, lwr, fwd
2	.50	500	Fus, lwr, aft
2	.50	500	Tail, tur

ELECTRONICS

VHF Command AN/ARC-3
Interphone AN/AIC-2A
Liaison AN/ARC-8
Radio Compass AN/ARN-7
Marker Beacon RC-193A
Homing Adapter AN/ARR-1
Localizer RC-103
Glide Path AN/ARN-5A
Radio Altimeter SCR-718C
Interrogator SCR-729
Radar . AN/APQ-7 or AN/APQ-23A
Loran . AN/APN-9 or AN/APN-4
IFF SCR-695
Raven .... RCM

Loading and Performance — Typical Mission

C O N D I T I O N S			BASIC MISSION	MAX BOMB	HIGH ALTITUDE	NORMAL WEIGHT	FERRY RANGE	
			I	II	III	IV	V	
TAKE-OFF WEIGHT		(lb)	140,000	140,000	140,000	133,500	138,278	
Fuel at 6.0 lb/gal (grade 100/130)		(lb)	47,196	39,396	47,196	41,496	56,178	
Payload (Bombs)		(lb)	10,000	20,000	10,000	10,000	None	
Wing loading		(lb/sq ft)	81.4	81.4	81.4	77.6	80.4	
Stall speed (power off)		(kn)	103	103	103	101	102	
Take-off ground run at SL	①	(ft)	5230	5230	5230	4575	5050	
Take-off to clear 50 ft	①	(ft)	7825	7825	7825	6765	7530	
Rate of climb at SL	②	(fpm)	500	500	500	585	520	
Rate of climb at SL (one engine out)	①	(fpm)	400	400	400	480	420	
Time: SL to 10,000 ft	②	(min)	20	20	20	18	19.5	
Time: SL to 20,000 ft	②	(min)	52	52	52	45	49	
Service ceiling (100 fpm)	②	(ft)	23,950	23,950	23,950	28,000	25,000	
Service ceiling (one engine out)	①	(ft)	19,400	19,400	19,400	23,800	20,650	
COMBAT RANGE	③	(n. mi.)	——	——	——	——	4809	
COMBAT RADIUS	③	(n. mi.)	1717	1384	1493	1523	——	
Average speed		(kn)	220	217	248	221	178	
Initial cruising altitude		(ft)	5000	5000	25,000	5000	5000	
Target speed		(kn)	312	298	312	314	——	
Target altitude		(ft)	30,000	25,000	30,000	30,000	——	
Final cruising altitude		(ft)	25,000	25,000	30,000	25,000	5000	
Total mission time		(hr)	15.35	12.77	12.22	13.5	27.03	
COMBAT WEIGHT		(lb)	101,082	96,815	98,862	98,550	82,400	
Combat altitude		(ft)	30,000	25,000	30,000	30,000	5000	
Combat speed	①	(kn)	347	333	348	348	282	
Combat climb	①	(fpm)	1120	1420	1185	1195	1650	
Combat ceiling (500 fpm)	①	(ft)	36,250	37,300	36,650	36,750	40,300	
Service ceiling (100 fpm)	②	(ft)	39,650	40,700	40,100	40,150	43,750	
Service ceiling (one engine out)	②	(ft)	34,800	36,200	35,400	35,550	39,650	
Max rate of climb at SL	①	(fpm)	1630	1770	1690	1700	2250	
Max speed at optimum altitude	①	(kn/ft)	347/30,000	348/30,000	348/30,000	348/30,000	353/30,000	
Basic speed at 25,000 ft		(kn)	331	333	332	332	339	
LANDING WEIGHT		(lb)	84,314	83,250	84,314	83,971	82,400	
Ground roll at SL		(ft)	2250	2225	2250	2245	2210	
Total from 50 ft		(ft)	2980	2950	2980	2975	2925	

NOTES
① Max power
② Normal power
③ Detailed descriptions of RADIUS and RANGE missions given on page 6.

PERFORMANCE BASIS:
(a) Data source: Flight test
(b) Performance is based on powers shown on page 6.

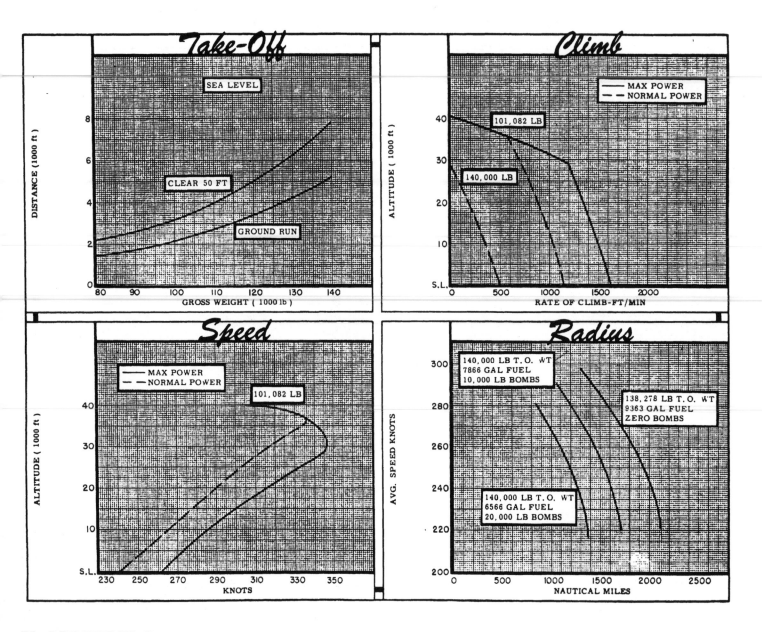

N O T E S

FORMULA: RADIUS MISSION I, II & IV

Warm-up, take-off, climb on course to 5000 ft at normal power, cruise at long range speeds at altitude for best range but not less than 5000 ft, climb on course to reach cruising ceiling 500 nautical miles from target, cruise in level flight to target including a 15 minutes normal bomb run, drop bombs and conduct 2 minutes evasive action (no distance credit) at combat altitude and an 8 minute run out from target with normal power, cruise at long range speeds at not less than combat altitude for 500 nautical miles, cruise back to base at long range speeds at not less than 5000 ft for best range. Range free allowances include 10 minutes normal power fuel consumption for warm-up and take-off, 2 minutes normal power fuel consumption at altitude for evasive action, and a landing reserve of 5% of initial fuel load plus fuel for 30 minutes for maximum endurance at sea level.

FORMULA: RADIUS MISSION III

Same as Radius Mission I except initial climb is to 25,000 ft.

FORMULA: RANGE MISSION V

Warm-up, take-off, climb on course to 5000 ft at normal power, cruise at long range speeds at altitude for best range but not less than 5000 ft. Range free allowances include 10 minutes normal power fuel consumption at sea level for warm-up and take-off, 5% of initial fuel load for landing reserve, plus 30 minutes fuel for maximum endurance at sea level.

GENERAL DATA:

(a) For detailed planning refer to Tech Order AN 01-20EJA-1

(b) Engine ratings shown on page 3 are manufacturer's guaranteed ratings. Power values used for performance calculations are as follows:

			(4) R-3350-57 or -57A	
	BHP	RPM	CRIT ALT*	MIN
T.O:	2200	2800		5
Max:	**2500	2600	31,400	30
Nor:	2000	2400	35,600	Cont.

* With Turbo
** As established by T.O. AN 01-20EJ-92 dated 15 June 1945.

(c) Bomb bay tanks are dropped when empty for all missions shown on page 4 except for ferry mission.

Loading and Performance—Typical Mission

CONDITIONS			BASIC MISSION
			I
TAKE-OFF WEIGHT		(lb)	140,000
Fuel at 6.0 lb/gal		(lb)	47,196
Military load (Bombs)		(lb)	10,000
Wing loading		(lb/sq ft)	81.4
Stall speed (power off)		(kn)	103
Take-off ground run at SL	①	(ft)	5230
Take-off to clear 50 ft	①	(ft)	7825
Rate-of-climb at SL	③	(fpm)	500
Time: SL to 10,000 ft	③	(min)	23.5
Time: SL to 20,000 ft	③	(min)	61.5
Service ceiling (100 fpm)	③	(ft)	23,950
Service ceiling (one engine out)	②	(ft)	19,400
COMBAT RANGE		(n. mi)	3445
Avg cruising speed		(kn)	198
Cruising altitude		(ft)	10,000
Total mission time		(hr)	17.54
COMBAT RADIUS		(n. mi)	1843
Avg cruising speed		(kn)	215
Cruising altitude (s)		(ft)	10,000 & 25,000
Total mission time		(hr)	17.37
COMBAT WEIGHT	④	(lb)	101,250
Combat altitude		(ft)	25,000
Combat speed	②	(kn)	331
Combat climb	②	(fpm)	1265
Combat ceiling (500 fpm)	②	(ft)	36,200
Service ceiling (100 fpm)	③	(ft)	39,600
Service ceiling (one engine out)	③	(ft)	34,700
Max rate-of-climb at SL	②	(fpm)	1625
Max speed at 30,000 ft	②	(kn)	347
LANDING WEIGHT		(lb)	83,564
Ground roll at SL		(ft)	2230
Total from 50 ft		(ft)	2960

1. Military Specification MIL-C-5011A dated 5 November 1951 redefines the combat radius to ground rules coordinated by the major USAF Air Commands and the Bureau of Aeronautics, U. S. Navy. Although in most cases the mission radius is reduced, this was considered to be more realistic based on Mission Profiles and Allowances proven in actual operation.

2. The combat radius for MIL-C-5011A is different from that based on MIL-C-5011 in that:

   a. Run into and out from the target area for high altitude bomber is at higher altitudes rather than at a specified altitude. This altitude corresponds to the cruise ceiling at the start of the combat zone, 500 n. mi. prior to target for reciprocating aircraft.

   b. Reserves are changed from a constant percentage of initial fuel as in MIL-C-5011 to a value equal to 5% of initial fuel load plus fuel for a specified period of 30 minutes long range at sea level.

   c. Combat range values are not quoted in MIL-C-5011A.

3. Certain items of performance quoted for MIL-C-5011A are different from those based on MIL-C-5011 in that:

   a. Time to climb values consider the effects of weight reduction during ground operation and climb.

   b. Average cruising speed does not include time and distance in climbs or target operation at normal power.

   c. Combat altitude is the altitude at which the actual target run is conducted.

   d. Basic speed is the maximum level flight speed within all operating limitations at the combat weight and at a specified altitude. This basic speed is quoted as a means of direct comparison of aircraft of similar type.

NOTES

① Take-off power
② Max power
③ Normal power
④ For Radius Mission

PERFORMANCE BASIS:
(a) Data source: Flight Tests

Loading and Performance — Typical Mission

CONDITIONS		BASIC MISSION
		I
TAKE-OFF WEIGHT	(lb)	132,750
Fuel at 6.0 lb/gal (grade 100/130)	(lb)	46,806
Military load (Boat) A-3 Rescue Boat	(lb)	3491
Wing loading	(lb/sq ft)	77.2
Stall speed (power off, landing configuration)	(kn)	100
Take-off ground run at SL ②	(ft)	4500
Take-off to clear 50 ft ②	(ft)	6650
Rate of climb at SL ③	(fpm)	500
Time: SL to 10,000 ft ③	(min)	23.5
Time: SL to 20,000 ft ③	(min)	62
Service Ceiling (100 fpm)	(ft)	22,000
COMBAT RANGE	(n. mi.)	3219
Average speed	(kn)	186
Initial cruising altitude	(ft)	10,000
Final cruising altitude	(ft)	10,000
Total mission time	(hr)	17.46
COMBAT RADIUS	(n. mi.)	1825
Average speed	(kn)	186
Initial cruising altitude	(ft)	10,000
Bombing altitude	(ft)	S.L.
Bomb run speed	(kn)	180
Final cruising altitude	(ft)	10,000
Total mission time	(hr)	19.75
COMBAT WEIGHT ④	(lb)	103,369
Combat altitude	(ft)	S.L.
Combat speed ①	(kn)	261
Combat climb ①	(fpm)	1570
Combat ceiling (500 fpm) ①	(ft)	35,750
Service ceiling (100 fpm) ①	(ft)	38,000
Max rate of climb at SL ①	(fpm)	1570
Max speed at 30,000 ft ①	(kn)	346
LANDING WEIGHT	(lb)	84,793
Ground roll at SL	(ft)	2250
Total from 50 ft	(ft)	2980

FORMULA: RADIUS MISSION

Warm-up, take-off, climb on course to 10,000 ft, cruise at long range speeds to point where descent is made to sea level drop boat, at long range speeds, climb on course to 10,000 ft and return to base at long range speeds. Range free allowances are 10 minutes normal power fuel consumption for warm-up and take-off plus 5% of initial fuel load for reserve.

FORMULA: RANGE MISSION

Same as outbound leg of radius mission continued until 90% of fuel has been used. Range free allowances include 10 minutes normal power fuel consumption for warm-up and take-off plus 10% of initial fuel load for reserve.

NOTES
① Max power (WE)
② T.O. power
③ Normal power
④ For Radius Mission if radius is shown.

PERFORMANCE BASIS:
(a) Data source: Flight test based on standard type B-29 airplane modified to include preliminary drag evaluation of A-3 life boat installation.

(b) This data will be revised in accordance with spec. MIL-C-5011A upon completion of flight test of SB-29.

NOTES

AUTHOR'S PERSPECTIVE

1. Peter M. Bowers, *Boeing Aircraft Since 1916* (London: Putnam, 1989), p. 318.

CHAPTER 1: THE B-29 SUPERFORTRESS

1. Named for its cofounder, William E. Boeing (1881–1956). He had established the firm as the Pacific Aero Products Company with Navy commander Conrad Westervelt.

2. Sikorsky left Russia during the civil war that followed World War I, eventually coming to the United States where he achieved fame as a seaplane designer and then as a pioneer in helicopter development.

3. The Army Air Corps was changed to Army Air Forces (AAF) on June 30, 1941.

4. The other members of the board were Lieutenant Colonel Carl Spaatz, Lieutenant Colonel Earl L. Naiden, and Major Alfred J. Lyon.

5. Allen was killed on February 18, 1943, in a crash of the second XB-29; ten engineers aboard the plane also were lost in the crash, and about 20 people were killed on the ground.

6. W. F. Craven and J. L. Cate, *The Pacific—Matterhorn to Nagasaki*, Vol. V of *The Army Air Forces in World War II* (Chicago: University of Chicago Press, 1953), p. 7.

7. Craven and Cate, *The Pacific*, pp. 22 passim.

8. Craven and Cate, *The Pacific*, p. 101.

9. Saipan and Tinian were Japanese possessions before World War II; Guam was a U.S. possession captured by Japanese troops on December 10, 1941.

10. Major General Curtis F. LeMay, USA, letter to General of the Army H. H. Arnold, USA, April 5, 1945. Paul Tibbets, commander of the 509th Composite Group, later wrote that he had proposed to LeMay the use of B-29s to firebomb Japanese cities as early as 1943; see Brigadier General Paul W. Tibbets, USAF, *The Tibbets Story* (New York: Stein and Day, 1978), pp. 188–189.

11. The 279 B-29 Superfortress bombers flying from bases in the Marina Islands dropped 1,665 tons of petroleum-based incendiaries on Tokyo. Japanese records show that 83,783 people were killed and some 100,000 were injured in that raid.

12. The Twentieth Air Force was established directly under the U.S. Joint Chiefs of Staff with General H. H. Arnold, head of the AAF, as nominal Twentieth Air Force commander. Arnold's staff in Washington assumed dual assignments, but in fact this was unsuccessful because of the burden on the staff.

CHAPTER 2: THE *ENOLA GAY*

1. The prefix 44 indicated that the aircraft was ordered in fiscal year 1944; 86292 was the sequential number of AAF aircraft ordered that year.

2. Wing loading is the aircraft's gross weight divided by the gross area of the wings.

3. The Wright R-3350 was first used in the single Douglas XB-19, which first flew in 1939. Less than 100 engines had been built when the R-3350 was selected for the mass-production B-29.

4. The M47 incendiaries were jellied gasoline, generally called napalm (for *naph*thene and *palm*itate), and consisted of gasoline and a thickening material.

5. The prefix AN indicated Army/Navy electronic equipment; the suffix letters indicated: A = Airborne, P = radar, Q = multipurpose, G = Gunnery.

6. Several German aircraft in World War II had remote-control guns, notably the He 111 and Me 210; however, they did not have a centralized fire-control system or the amount of firepower or sophistication of the B-29.

7. Lieutenant General Leslie R. Groves, USA, *Now It Can Be Told: The Story of the Manhattan Project* (New York: Harper, 1962), p. 256n.

8. The Tallboy and Grand Slam were so-called earthquake bombs, designed by Dr. Barnes Wallis of Vickers-Armstrong (Aircraft) to destroy subterranean targets such as bridge and viaduct foundations, with the bombs creating shock waves. The Tallboy was also used to attack the German battleship *Tirpitz* at anchor.

9. In fact, the German's surprise offensive (Battle of the Bulge) in late December 1944 delayed the Allied victory in Europe. Germany surrendered to the Allies in the first week of May 1945.

10. Tibbets, *The Tibbets Story*, p. 155.

11. Organizational data from Groves, *Now It Can Be Told*, and "History of the 509th Composite Group, 313rd Bombardment Wing, Twentieth Air Force, Activation to 15 Aug 1945"; manuscript at Air University Library, Maxwell Air Force Base, Alabama. Eventually, the 509th Composite Group had an authorized strength of 205 officers and 1,624 enlisted men.

12. When the 509th Composite Group began to deploy overseas in May 1945, the 320th Troop Carrier Squadron traded in its four C-47s for additional C-54s.

13. The third major island in the Marianas was Guam, which had been a U.S. possession before World War II. The Japanese had captured it with little opposition in early December 1941. It was recaptured by U.S. troops and declared secure on August 10, 1944.

14. The letter from Admiral E. J. King, Commander-in-Chief U.S. Fleet, was delivered personally to Admiral Nimitz by Commander Frederick L. Ashworth, who would fly as weapons officer on the Nagasaki atomic bomb mission.

CHAPTER 3: THE MISSION

1. The Quonset hut was a widely used structure, produced in the tens of thousands for U.S. and Allied forces during the war. A half-cylindrical design made of corrugated metal, the Quonset hut was used for offices, hospitals, barracks, and warehouses. The first huts were built for the U.S. Navy in 1941 at Quonset Point, Rhode Island. The design was a modification of the British-produced Nissen Hut.

2. The origins of the circle-arrow insignia are not recorded. The insignia was originally just an arrowhead. Most B-29s carried a geometric symbol for the wing and letter for the group. Historian Dana Bell of the National Air and Space Museum believes that the arrowhead may have been an attempt to disguise the 509th aircraft as being assigned to an air depot unit.

3. Tibbets, *The Tibbets Story*, p. 190.

4. See Groves, *Now It Can Be Told*, pp. 268–276, for a discussion of the target selection criteria and process.

5. General H. H. Arnold later wrote in his autobiography, *Global Mission* (New York: Harper & Brothers, 1949), "[Secretary of War Henry] Stimson struck off my list the city of Kyoto. Kyoto had a population of 752,000 and was an important manufacturing center. In my opinion it should have been destroyed. But the Secretary said it was one of the holy cities of the world, and of outstanding religious significance."

6. The last major B-29 raid on Tokyo, on the night of May 25–26, 1945, did damage the Imperial Palace. During that massive incendiary raid, flaming debris from the fires hurdled across the moat of the Imperial Palace, which was initially constructed in 1888. Despite the best efforts of some 10,000 firefighters, troops, and government workers to extinguish the flames, 27 palace buildings were destroyed in less than four hours. Twenty-eight members of the imperial staff were killed in the flames, while the Emperor, Empress, and their senior attendants cowered in a newly built bomb shelter beneath the palace library.

7. U.S. Army, Foreign Radio Reports, July 21, 1945.

8. Nine aircraft were scheduled to make the latter strike, but the Pumpkin in one aircraft broke loose from the bomb shackles and fell through the closed bomb bay doors. There was no explosion or fire, despite a shower of sparks as the bomb scraped along the paved taxi strip. No one was injured. This and the detonating of two Pumpkin bombs too

soon after their release were the only accidents suffered by the 509th in the forward area.

9. From General Thomas T. Handy, USA, to General Carl Spaatz, USA, July 25, 1945.

10. David McCullough, *Truman* (New York: Simon & Schuster, 1992), p. 448.

11. General Groves later remarked that the *Indianapolis* "was a very poor choice to carry the bomb. She had no underwater sound equipment [sonar], and was so designed that a single torpedo was able to sunk her quickly" (Groves, *Now It Can Be Told*, p. 306). Actually, two torpedoes struck the ship.

12. Harlow W. Russ, *Project Alberta: The Preparation of Atomic Bombs for Use in World War II* (Los Alamos, N.M.: Exceptional Books, 1984), p. 59.

13. Russ, *Project Alberta*, p. 59.

14. Russ, *Project Alberta*, p. 60.

15. *The Great Artiste* was named for Captain Kermit K. Beahan, the aircraft's bombardier.

16. Major Sweeney previously commanded the 320th Troop Carrier Squadron; he took command of the 393rd Heavy Bombardment Squadron in March 1945.

17. Cited in Al Christman, *Target Hiroshima: Deak Parsons and the Creation of the Atomic Bomb* (Annapolis, Md.: Naval Institute Press, 1998), p. 2.

18. This time was one hour ahead of the time in Hiroshima.

19. The Hiroshima bomb missed the aim point by about 500 feet.

20. Estimates of the Hiroshima and Nagasaki bomb yields vary considerably; the numbers used here are from the definitive analysis by John Malik of the Los Alamos National Laboratory in his *The Yields of the Hiroshima and Nagasaki Nuclear Explosions* (Los Alamos, N.M.: September, 1985). Among the dead at Hiroshima were several American prisoners of war. Tibbets notes in his book *The Tibbets Story* that the location of prisoner of war camps had been involved in the selection of target cities, but no major prisoner camp or holding area was identified at Hiroshima. After the war, it was learned that 23 fliers were held captive in Hiroshima when it was destroyed (p. 196).

21. Jacob Beser. *Hiroshima and Nagasaki Revisited* (Memphis, Tenn.: Global Press, 1988), p. 112. Beser wrote, "The fighter pulled up along side, dropped his wheels and flaps to slow down, looked us over, slow rolled around us, then sped away." The *Enola Gay* and other B-29s of the 509th Composite Group mounted only tail guns.

22. Tokyo was 13 hours ahead of Washington, the latter being on Eastern War Time.

23. Statement of August 6, 1945, in *Public Papers of the Presidents: Harry S. Truman, 1945* (Washington, D.C.: Government Printing Office, 1961), p. 199.

24. Some official documents refer to the amount of fuel that could not be used at 800 gallons; however, the 600-gallon figure appears more likely.

25. The aircraft was named for Captain Fred C. Bock; he and his crew flew *The Great Artiste* (instrument aircraft) on the Nagasaki bombing mission.

26. Beser, *Hiroshima and Nagasaki*, p. 5.

27. Interview with unknown source; date unknown (in *Enola Gay* files at National Air and Space Museum, Washington, D.C.).

28. Laurence won the Pulitzer Prize for his reporting of the atomic bomb strikes.

29. At that point *Bockscar* had an estimated 1,200 gallons of usable fuel remaining—enough to reach Nagasaki and, without the weight of the bomb, fly on to Okinawa.

30. The Nagasaki bomb missed its aim point by about a mile and a half.

CHAPTER 4: B-29 POSTSCRIPTS

1. Tibbets, *The Tibbets Story*, p. 242.

2. Joint Chiefs of Staff, January 11, 1946; reprinted in W. A. Shurcliff, *Bombs at Bikini: The Official Report of Operation Crossroads* (New York: William H. Wise, 1947), p. 14.

3. About this time the 509th was redesignated as the 509th Bombardment Group.

4. Letter from Major General LeMay to Commanding General, Strategic Air Command, subject: Mission of the 58th Bombardment Wing, June 13, 1946.

5. The U.S. Air Force was created as a separate service on September 18, 1947, replacing the U.S. Army Air Forces.

6. The Navy designation P2B indicated *Patrol*, the *2nd* aircraft of that type built by *Boeing*; the name Superfortress was retained. The Navy planes were ex–Air Force B-29s, acquired in 1947.

7. The project was sponsored by Westinghouse Electric Corporation and the Glenn L. Martin Company.

8. An ex-Navy, twin-engine Lockheed PV-2C Harpoon was employed in Stratovision tests from December 1945 to August 1946.

9. At the time one B-29 squadron from the 301st Bomb Group was on rotational training at Furstenfeldbruck, West Germany.

10. Lewis L. Strauss, *Men and Decisions* (London: Macmillan, 1963), p. 205.

11. Robert F. Furtell, *The United States Air Force in Korea 1950–1953* (New York: Duell, Sloan and Pearce, 1961), p. 27.

12. Although ostensibly piloted by Chinese, many of the MiG-15s were flown by Soviet Air Forces pilots.

13. The Victor, Valiant, and Vulcan.

14. The first British nuclear weapon was the Blue Danube bomb, which became operational in July 1955.

15. The Tu-4 story is told in L. L. Kerber, *Stalin's Aviation Gulag: A Memoir of Andrei Tupolev and the Purge Era* (Washington, D.C.: Smithsonian Institution Press, 1996), pp. 255–271; and Von Hardesty, "Made in the U.S.S.R.," *Air & Space* (February/March 2001): pp. 68–79. Hardesty, a curator at the National Air and Space Museum, was editor of the Kerber book.

16. GAZ = *Gosudarstvennyy Aviatsionnyy Zavod* (state aviation factory).

17. Bill Gunston, *Tupolev Aircraft Since 1922* (London: Putnam, 1995), p. 128.

18. The AEW aircraft was retired to the Datangshan aviation museum near Xiao Tang San, near Beijing; another Tu-4 on exhibit at the museum is configured for carrying unmanned aerial vehicles under its wings.

CHAPTER 5: THE ARTIFACT

1. The *NC-4* was the world's first aircraft to fly across the Atlantic, in May 1919.

2. Interview with Lin Ezell, filmed at Garber facility, 1995.

3. Interview with Timothy Howard, student at Parks Air College, St. Louis, Mo., filmed at Garber facility, 1995.

4. Guernica was the site of a savage German bombing attack in 1937 during the Spanish Civil War. The attack was immortalized by Pablo Picasso in his painting *Guernica*, done the same year.

5. The film, produced in 1995 by the Greenwich Workshop, is on sale in the museum shop.

BIBLIOGRAPHY

Allen, Thomas B., and Norman Polmar. *Codename Downfall: The Secret Plan to Invade Japan and Why Truman Used the Bomb*. New York: Simon & Schuster, 1995.

Arnold, Gen. Air Force H. H. *Global Mission*. New York: Harper & Brothers, 1949.

Beser, Jacob. *Hiroshima and Nagasaki Revisited*. Memphis, Tenn.: Global Press, 1988.

Birdsall, Steve. *Saga of the Superfortress: The Dramatic Story of the B-29 and the Twentieth Air Force*. New York: Doubleday, 1980.

Bowers, Peter M. *Boeing Aircraft Since 1916*. London: Putnam, 1989.

Christman, Al. *Target: Deak Parsons and the Creation of the Atomic Bomb*. Annapolis, Md.: Naval Institute Press, 1998.

Craven, W. F., and J. L. Cate. *Men and Planes*, Vol. VI of *The Army Air Forces in World War II*. Chicago: University of Chicago Press, 1955.

———. *The Pacific Matterhorn to Nagasaki*, Vol. V of *The Army Air Forces in World War II*. Chicago: University of Chicago Press, 1953.

Davis, Larry. *B-29 Superfortress in Action*. Carrollton, Tex.: Squadron/Signal Publications, 1997.

Dorr, Robert F. *B-29 Superfortress Units of World War II*. Botley, Oxford: Osprey, 2002.

Furtell, Robert F. *The United States Air Force in Korea 1950–1953*. New York: Duell, Sloan and Pearce, 1961.

Gunston, Bill. *Tupolev Aircraft Since 1922*. London: Putnam, 1995.

Groves, Lieutenant General Leslie R., USA. *Now It Can Be Told: The Story of the Manhattan Project*. New York: Harper, 1962.

Harwit, Martin. *An Exhibit Denied: Lobbying the History of the Enola Gay*. New York: Copernicus, 1996.

Kerber, L. L. *Stalin's Aviation Gulag: A Memoir of Andrei Tupolev and the Purge Era*. Washington, D.C.: Smithsonian Institution Press, 1996.

Knaack, Marcelle Size. *Post–World War II Bombers 1945–1973*, Vol. II of *Encyclopedia of U.S. Air Force Aircraft and Missile Systems*. Washington, D.C.: Office of Air Force History, 1988.

Knebel, Fletcher, and Charles W. Bailey II. *No High Ground*. New York: Harper & Brothers, 1960.

Laurence, William L. *Dawn over Zero: The Story of the Atomic Bomb*. New York: Alfred A. Knopf, 1946.

LeMay, Gen. Curtis E., USAF, and Bill Yenne. *Superfortress: The B-29 and American Air Power*. New York: McGraw-Hill, 1988.

Malik, John. *The Yields of the Hiroshima and Nagasaki Nuclear Explosions*. Los Alamos, N.M.: Los Alamos National Laboratory, 1985.

McCullough, David. *Truman*. New York: Simon & Schuster, 1992.

Meulen, Jacob Vander. *Building the B-29*. Washington, D.C.: Smithsonian Institution Press, 1995.

Norris, Robert Standish. *Racing for the Bomb: General Leslie R. Groves, the Manhattan Project's Indispensable Man*. South Royalton, Vt.: Steerforth Press, 2002.

Polmar, Norman, and Lieutenant Colonel Tim Laur, USAF (Ret.). *Strategic Air Command: People, Aircraft, and Missiles*. Baltimore, Md.: Nautical and Aviation Publishing, 1990.

Rhodes, Richard. *The Making of the Atomic Bomb*. New York: Simon & Schuster, 1988.

Russ, Harlow W. *Project Alberta: The Preparation of Atomic Bombs for Use in World War II*. Los Alamos, N.M.: Exceptional Books, 1984.

Shurcliff, W. A. *Bombs at Bikini: The Official Report of Operation Crossroads*. New York: William H. Wise, 1947.

Strauss, Rear Adm. Lewis L., USN (Ret.). *Men and Decisions*. London: Macmillan, 1963.

Tibbets, Brigadier General Paul W., USAF. *The Tibbets Story*. New York: Stein and Day, 1978.

U.S. Department of State. *Public Papers of the Presidents: Harry S. Truman, 1945*. Washington, D.C.: Government Printing Office, 1961.

Werrell, Kenneth P. *Blankets of Fire: U.S. Bombers over Japan during World War II*. Washington, D.C.: Smithsonian Institution Press, 1996.

In addition, the author made use of articles in the following journals:

Air International (U.K.)
Air and Space (U.S.)
American Aviation Historical Society Journal (U.S.)
Aviation Week & Space Technology (U.S.)
Flight (U.K.)
Flying Review International (U.K.)
Military Parade (Russia)

INDEX

(Ranks indicated are the highest used in the text.)

Trinity: *see* atomic bomb, first test
Truman, Harry S., 26, 27, 33, 35, 43, 51
Tu-4 bomber, 55–58
Tu-70 aircraft, 55
Tupolev, Andrei N., 55, 57

U-2 aircraft, 55
Udvar-Hazy, Steven F., 64
Udvar-Hazy Center, 63, 64

Van Kirk, Capt. Theodore J., 26, 31, 32, 33
Vautour, operation, 54

Washington bomber, 55
Wings
    58th Bombardment, 46
    313rd Bombardment, 4, 23

X-1 aircraft, 47–49

Y1B-9 bomber, 1
Y1B-17 bomber, 2
Yeager, Charles E., 48

ABOUT THE AUTHOR

Norman Polmar is an analyst, consultant, and author specializing in aviation, naval, and intelligence issues. He has written or coauthored more than 30 books and numerous articles in these fields. In 1997–1998, he held the Ramsey Chair of Naval Aviation History at the National Air and Space Museum in Washington, D.C.

Mr. Polmar has been a consultant to several senior officials in the Navy and Department of Defense and has directed several studies for U.S. and foreign shipbuilding and aerospace firms. From 1982 to 1986 and since December 2003 he has been a member of the Secretary of the Navy's Research Advisory Committee (NRAC). He was also a consultant to the director of the Los Alamos National Laboratory and a panel member of the Naval Studies Board of the National Academy of Sciences. Mr. Polmar has served as a consultant to three U.S. senators and two members of the House of Representatives and as a consultant or advisor to three Secretaries of the Navy and two Chiefs of Naval Operations.

Prior to 1980, Mr. Polmar was an executive and, before that, an analyst with research firms specializing in strategic, submarine, and naval issues.

With Thomas B. Allen he is coauthor of *Codename Downfall: The Secret Plan to Invade Japan and Why Truman Used the Bomb* (1995). Mr. Polmar's other aviation books include *Aircraft Carriers: A History of Carrier Aviation and Its Influence on World Events* (1969), *World Combat Aircraft Directory* (1976), *Military Helicopters of the World* with Floyd D. Kennedy (1981), *The Naval Air War in Vietnam* with Peter B. Mersky (1981), and *Spyplane: U-2 History Declassified* (2001).